Amelia Earhart

Amelia
Earhart

Tanya Lee Stone

DK PUBLISHING

LONDON, NEW YORK, MUNICH,
MELBOURNE, and DELHI

Editor : Alisha Niehaus
Publishing Director : Beth Sutinis
Designer : Mark Johnson Davies
Senior Designer : Tai Blanche
Art Director : Dirk Kaufman
Photo Research : Anne Burns Images
Production : Ivor Parker
DTP Designer : Kathy Farias

First American Edition, 2007

07 08 09 10 11 10 9 8 7 6 5 4 3 2 1
Published in the United States
by DK Publishing
375 Hudson Street, New York,
New York 10014

DK books are available at special discounts
when purchased in bulk for sales promotions,
premiums, fund-raising, or educational use.
For details, contact:

DK Publishing Special Markets
375 Hudson Street
New York, New York 10014
SpecialSales@dk.com

A catalog record for this book is available
from the Library of Congress.

Printed and bound in China
by South China Printing Co., Ltd.

Photography credits:
Front cover: © Corbis/Bettman
Back Cover: © Corbis

Discover more at
www.dk.com

Contents

Note: Although it is customary to refer to people by their last names in biographies, it did not feel natural here. Amelia was too fun-loving and adventurous.

A Shooting Star

This commemorative stamp was issued to honor Earhart in 1963.

On July 2, 1937, headlines shocked the world. Amelia Earhart, internationally known, record-breaking female aviator, had disappeared. She had been attempting to be the first woman pilot to fly around the world, and was almost at the end of her trip when her plane vanished in the Pacific. There are many theories as to what happened to her and her navigator Fred Noonan, but to this day their plane has not been found. Did they crash into the ocean? Drown? Were they picked up by the Japanese and held as prisoners of war? Had Amelia been on a spy mission for the U.S. military? After an extensive search, the world came to terms with the fact that their golden girl was gone. But there was never any proof of what became of her.

Amelia Earhart was like a shooting star. She burned fast and bright, and faded from sight too quickly. But her memory lives on. Who was this woman who has become the stuff of legends? Scholarly books disagree on many details of her life, for she was an intensely private person when it came to personal matters. Perhaps for that reason, historians have had to piece her story together from many different sources—

all of which bring their own perspective to the table. In addition, the information Amelia did provide was not always accurate. At some point, she started saying she was born in 1898 instead of 1897. She also fudged some information on at least one job application. And although she wrote books about her life, they focused primarily on her flying career.

Still, in looking at a person's life, one must do more than simply compile a list of facts. The task is to try and capture some of the essence of who that person really was. What made her tick? What drove her to do the things she did? What, and who, did she really care about? For Amelia Earhart, what stands out most is *how* she lived her life. Fearlessly. Unashamedly. And compassionately. She was a woman who took care of the people she loved, while still managing to live her life exactly as she chose to, by nobody else's rules. That makes her star shine brightly, and explains why, after all these years, we are still fascinated by her story.

Amelia captured America's heart with her adventurous spirit and passion for flying.

chapter 1

A Tomboy by Nature

In a house 400 feet (122 m) above the waters of the Missouri River, in Atchison, Kansas, Amy Earhart was about to have a baby. She had traveled from Kansas City, where she and her husband Edwin lived, so she could give birth at her mother's house. There, Amy could rest and have the support of nearby family and friends. A week-long heat wave likely made Amy more uncomfortable than ever. Thankfully, the insufferable heat finally gave way to a lightning storm, followed by a cooling torrential downpour. When the air

The Otis home in Atchison, Kansas, is now the site of an Amelia Earhart museum.

cleared, a starry sky ushered in the arrival of Amy's daughter. Amelia Mary Earhart, a healthy baby girl of 9 pounds (4 kg), was born at 11:30 p.m. on July 24, 1897. She was named for both her grandmothers—Amelia Otis and Mary Earhart.

It is fitting that Amelia and Alfred Otis welcomed their granddaughter into their home on the day she was born, as she would live with her grandparents on and off throughout

Amelia was born in her grandparents' home and spent much of her childhood there.

her childhood. Atchison was up-and-coming in the 1880s, and Alfred Otis was one of the wealthiest and most prestigious members of the community. Amy had grown up accustomed to the lifestyle her father's status provided, which included being waited on by servants and spending her time as she pleased. She met Edwin Earhart at her coming-out party, when she was sixteen. It was love at first sight. Edwin was handsome, smart, and charming. He was also fairly poor, though, and not of a high enough social standing, in Alfred Otis's opinion.

Although Alfred disapproved of his daughter's

9

Amelia's parents—Amy and Edwin Earhart—on their wedding day.

relationship with Edwin, Amy was not swayed. She kept after her father until he came up with a test: Alfred would let Amy marry Edwin once he got a job making at least 50 dollars per month, proving he could provide for Amy. It took Edwin five years to achieve this goal, but he did it, working as a claims lawyer for a railroad company.

He and Amy were married in October 1895. The newlyweds then moved to Kansas City, into a house that had been bought—and furnished—for them by Amy's father.

Unfortunately, although Amy and Edwin loved each other, there were signs that Alfred's suspicions about Edwin had been right. Edwin was in financial trouble by 1903, having squandered his money on an invention patent that fell through instead of paying taxes on the family's home. He seemed to spend money as quickly as he made it, which was curious since Alfred Otis had already paid for many of the couple's biggest expenses, such as their house. But Edwin was a loving father from the start, spending so much time with Amelia that her first word was "Papa."

When Amelia was three, her little sister Muriel was born. Amy Earhart, who was already working harder than she was

accustomed to, sent Amelia to live in Atchison with her grandparents for a while. Amelia was a lively child and Amy thought her daughter could do wonders to help lift Amelia Otis's spirits. There had been losses in the close-knit family, and Amelia would be a breath of fresh air for her grandmother.

Amelia had her own room at the house in Atchison, overlooking the river. Her mother visited often, and Amelia returned to Kansas City in the summers. This might have been a difficult arrangement for another child—moving back and forth between two homes. But Amelia seemed to thrive in both places. Her grandparents had a large library and Amelia loved to read whatever she could get her hands on. She made great friends, teaching several of them how to ride a bike, and loved to explore the caves by the river bank, make up adventure stories in the barn, as well as play "big game hunter" and other daring games. As one childhood friend later recalled, "Amelia was more fun to play with than

From right to left, this family portrait shows Alfred Otis, Amelia, Muriel, Amelia's aunt Annie, and Amelia Otis holding baby Otis in her lap.

anyone else." Amelia's grandmother disapproved of her "tomboy" behavior, but Amelia found ways around that. She was careful, for example, only to jump the fence when her grandmother was not looking!

Back in Kansas City, Amelia's parents had much more lenient ideas about what girls could and couldn't do. Pidge (as Amelia called Muriel) and Meely (as Muriel called Amelia) had little interest in games such as make-believe tea parties. They wanted to play games commonly thought of as "boy" activities, such as baseball and football—and their parents encouraged them. Amy even had play suits made for them, which, Amelia later wrote, "shocked all the nice little girls." Amelia loved to ride horses and she collected specimens such as dead insects, spiders, and even a cow's skull. The sisters had worm races, complete with tiny harnesses made of grass.

When Amelia got too wild, Amy did draw the line.

Muriel (climbing the swing rope) and Amelia (on stilts) in their homemade play suits.

For example, when Amelia was seven, her mother made her take apart an exciting but rather hazardous roller coaster she had built in the yard!

Amelia's father adored spending time with his girls. Edwin could often be found playing "cowboys and indians" with them, taking them fishing, or making up exciting stories to dazzle them and their friends. One Christmas, Edwin gave the girls sleds. In those days, girls used short sleds on

Amelia loved to play outdoors and learned to ride a horse at a young age. Here, she is 10 years old.

which they were to ride sitting politely upright, while boys had longer, stronger sleds they could go "bellywhopping" on for greater speed—and fun. When Amelia opened the large package that Christmas morning, she must have been overjoyed to find one of these longer sleds. Going fast was something she particularly loved, and zipping down an icy hill offered the thrill and speed she was looking for. That "boy" sled may even have saved her life, as the story goes.

One wintry day, Amelia was nearing the bottom of a hill on her sled when a horse and cart turned the corner, headed right across her path. There was no time to turn, and the driver didn't see her in time to stop. Incredibly,

Amelia and her sled slipped right under the horse and out the other side. As Amelia stated later, "Had I been sitting up, either my head or the horse's ribs would have suffered in contact."

Edwin was an entertaining and playful father, and he kept his troubles to himself as often as possible. But his bad habit of spending money he didn't have would interfere with his family life on and off for years. In hope of getting out of debt, Edwin took a different job within the railroad company, which involved a transfer from Kansas City to Des Moines, Iowa. Amy went with her husband to look for a house, and Amelia returned to her grandparents' home. This time, Muriel went, too. They

This photo shows the Iowa State Fair in 1911, just a few years after Amelia went.

joined their parents nearly a year later.

Around this time, Edwin took the family to the Iowa state fair. Amelia was 11 years old and saw her first airplane at the fair, although it didn't make much of an impression on her. She remembered, "It was a thing of rusty wire and wood and not at all interesting."

The family's first few years in Iowa seemed happy, but trouble was brewing in Edwin. Perhaps it was Alfred Otis's constant disapproval, or perhaps it was always being on the brink of financial troubles. For whatever reasons, Edwin began to drink. He also began to change from somewhat irresponsible but fun-loving into an erratic, unreliable man whose employer no longer trusted him. Eventually, Edwin lost his job with the railroad company. And the girls, who used to delight in his company, stayed out of his way more and more.

December 17, 1903

Five years before Amelia Earhart saw her first plane at the Iowa State Fair, Wilbur and Orville Wright made history by taking to the sky in an airplane of their own design. It was the first powered, piloted flight—ever. Windy and hilly Kitty Hawk, North Carolina, was the perfect place to launch their flying machine. They had tested their 50-pound (23 kg) biplane glider there in 1900, and the brothers returned in 1903 to fly their 700-pound (318 kg) motored plane, which they called *The Flyer*. On the third attempt, made on December 17, Orville flew *The Flyer* for 12 seconds, and history was made.

chapter 2

A High-Spirited Girl

When Amelia's grandmother Amelia Otis died in 1911, the Earharts stood to inherit a lot of money. Surely, this would help get them back on their feet while Edwin was struggling. But Amelia Otis took her distrust of Edwin to the grave, believing he would squander any money that made its way into his hands. In an effort to protect the wealth being left to her daughter Amy, Amelia Otis stipulated that the funds could not be touched for 20 years—unless Edwin died before the time was up. Edwin was furious. His drinking grew worse and no one would hire him. For a while he simply went off on his own, leaving his family. It's not clear whether the girls were aware of this, as their mother explained his absence as the result of a long business trip.

Eventually, however, he did come back, and in 1913 finally found another, albeit lesser, job. This one was in St. Paul, Minnesota, and the house he bought there was a step down, as well. Once

Edwin Earhart's troubles had a negative impact on the young lives of his daughters.

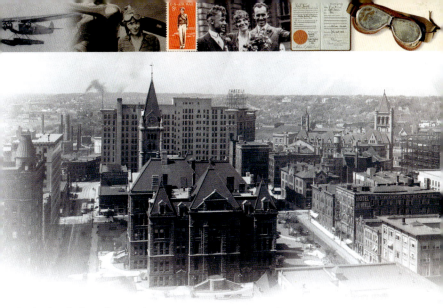

This is the skyline of St. Paul, Minnesota, around the time Amelia's family lived there.

again, Amelia had to move to a new city, attend a new school, and make new friends. But Amelia prided herself on adapting well to situations. She later wrote: "I have never lived more than four years in any one place and always have to ask 'Which one?' when a stranger greets me by saying, 'I'm from your home town.'"

She did not adapt as easily to her father's situation, though. He had supposedly stopped drinking, but when Amelia helped pack his suitcase for a business trip she found he had tucked a whiskey bottle in among his clothing. She emptied it in the sink. In a rare show of violence, Edwin yelled and raised his hand to his daughter. Amy stopped him, and he apologized for what he had almost done. This incident, as well as several others in which Edwin was supposed to meet his daughters and either failed to show up, or showed up drunk, colored how Amelia saw her father.

17

In 1914, the family moved to Springfield, Missouri, with the promise of yet another job. Upon arrival, however, Edwin discovered there had been some confusion and there was no permanent job for him after all. Instead, the company offered him a month of temporary work and he moved his family into a boarding house. Amy Earhart had had enough.

Amy told Edwin she was leaving—and taking the girls with her. She contacted friends in Chicago, who invited them to stay until they found a place of their own. With this safety net, Amy found rooms to rent in an apartment in Hyde Park owned by two older women. As a woman at this time, it is likely Amy would not have been able to afford taking even this step on her own if she had not

Years later, in 1928, Amelia returned to her Hyde Park high school to speak to the students.

had rights to the interest earned from the money her mother had left her.

Amelia was 17 when she got to Chicago. Her relationship with her father was troubled, her family's social standing was crumbling, and she had yet another school in which to carve out her own way. Not surprisingly, Amelia's happy-go-lucky disposition transformed somewhat into a quiet determination. She had a strong sense of self and was not about to

As a teen whose family moved around a lot, Amelia grew skilled at adapting to new situations.

let anyone else's actions affect what she thought or did. This attitude showed up in a letter written to a friend in 1914. In the letter, it is clear that Amelia was aware of the changes in her family's status but that this had not put a damper on her own goals. She wrote: "Of course I'm going to Bryn Mawr if I have to drive a grocery wagon to accumulate the cash." Most of the time, however, Amelia kept her family troubles to herself.

Amelia's experience at Hyde Park High School was much different than at her past schools. She chose it because it was the best public school in Chicago, but unlike at previous schools, she did not develop a social life there. She studied hard and became a loner, not making any new friends. Perhaps this was her way of getting through a final year of being unsettled beyond her control. She had, after all, been to six high schools in four years. Amelia didn't even go to her own high school graduation in 1915, and the caption that accompanied her senior photograph read: "The girl in brown who walks alone."

Once Amelia had finished high school, Amy decided it was time to reunite with Edwin. He seemed to have gotten his life back in order and was living in Kansas City with his sister, once again practicing law. Amelia still loved her father, but it's unlikely she was overjoyed at the prospect of living as a family again. She intended to go off to college preparatory school and start an independent life.

When Amy's brother Mark died, Edwin convinced her it was time to challenge her mother's

Amelia (on left) stands with two friends at the Ogontz School.

will again. Unfortunately, they discovered that Mark had lost most of the family fortune in bad investments, but they were able to scrape together enough money to send Muriel and Amelia to the schools of their choice. Muriel went to St. Margaret's in Toronto and Amelia went to the Ogontz School in Philadelphia, still planning to go on to nearby Bryn Mawr after that.

Amelia was 19 when she started at Ogontz in the fall of 1916. There, she was somewhat back to her old self—perhaps a bit less carefree—making new friends and enjoying herself fully for the first time in what must have seemed like a long time. She got good grades, played field hockey and basketball, and indulged in other favorite, quirky habits such as climbing onto the roof at night or intentionally misspelling words in her papers as a means of playing with language. She heard the Philadelphia Symphony play and went to the theater. It was at this time Amelia began noticing the achievements of various women whenever they were mentioned in newspapers or magazines. She even started a scrapbook of clippings to preserve and honor their accomplishments.

When the term was over, Amelia headed to Kansas City for a brief visit with her family, and then to Camp Gray on the shores of Lake Michigan where she spent the summer with friends. Edwin took her part of the way, and a letter home to her mother indicates the complexity of her feelings for her father: "Poppy was such a lamb last night I came near coming back to him."

chapter **3**

Finding Her Way

Back at Ogontz, Amelia immersed herself in student life, heaping several extracurricular responsibilities on top of her school work. She became increasingly popular, respected for always taking the high road and speaking out against injustices whenever she noticed them. She was elected vice president of her class, as well as secretary of the school's chapter of the Red Cross. Her classmates also asked her to write their senior song. Amelia was aware that she was taking on a lot, and just as aware of her competence. In a letter to her mother, she wrote: "you know the more one does the more one can do."

Sources differ regarding this photo. It has been described both as a snapshot of Amelia in a Halloween costume at Ogontz, and as a high school graduation portrait.

One of the causes she took up on campus was related to the recent U.S. entry into World War I (1914–1918). American troops had gone overseas in June 1917. The school's Red Cross chapter was already knitting sweaters for soldiers and donating money

earned through a food drive. Amelia wanted to find another way to raise funds. In an effort to convince her classmates that they should pool the dollars about to be spent on expensive class rings and use it to help the war effort, she appealed to her fellow students: "We others are only asking [that] we turn our money to the Red Cross and have only a little gold band." This was a small gesture that was a sign of bigger things to come.

At Christmastime, Amelia traveled to Toronto to visit her sister.

World War I (1914–1918)

At the turn of the century, there was a delicate balance of power in Europe and tensions were on the rise. In 1914, World War I erupted when Austria-Hungary, after securing Germany's support, declared war on Serbia. Russia leapt to Serbia's defense and Germany declared war on Russia. Other countries soon took sides, joining either the Allied Powers (Russia's side) or the Central Powers (Germany's side). Britain (and by extension, Canada) joined the Allies after Germany invaded Belgium, since Britain was the official protector of Belgium's neutrality. America tried to stay neutral, but joined the Allies after its relationship with Germany crumbled. The final blow occurred when the Germans torpedoed two American ships in March 1917. World War I finally ended on November 11, 1918.

Their mother joined this reunion. Canada had been involved with the conflict in Europe since the beginning, and the harsh reality of war was painfully obvious as Amelia walked the Toronto streets. She was stunned to see "men without arms and legs, men who were paralyzed and men who were blind. One day I saw four one-legged men at once, walking as best they

could down the street together," she later wrote. For Amelia, there was only one choice—to stay and help.

At her mother's urging, Amelia did return to Ogontz to finish her studies, but she could not bring herself to remain there. By February, she told her mother she had to quit school. The diploma was not what mattered to her. She had learned a lot at Ogontz and was ready to move on to the next thing she felt called to do. In her book *20 Hrs., 40 Min.,* Amelia would write: "There is so much that must be done in a civilized barbarism like war." Amy Earhart knew as well as anyone that when Amelia made up her mind to do something, there was no stopping her. Amelia withdrew from Ogontz and moved to Toronto, becoming a nurse's aid at the Spadina Military Hospital. She often worked from 7 a.m. to 7 p.m. Of course, Amelia also made time to make friends and have adventures. She even found time to go on dates and ride horses at a local stable.

One day, some Royal Canadian Air Force pilots were also riding. They were impressed with how Amelia handled an extremely difficult horse named Dynamite and invited her out to the airfield. Although her first exposure to an airplane all those years ago at the Iowa

Amelia poses in the traditional white uniform of a student nurse.

State Fair had not inspired her, now she was blown away. In her book *The Fun of It*, Amelia wrote: "No civilian had opportunity of going up. But I hung around in spare time and absorbed all I could."

If she hadn't already been completely enamored with flight, the deal was clinched when she went to a particularly exciting air show in Toronto.

Amelia sits astride her favorite horse, Dynamite.

One of the pilots had apparently gotten bored, or wanted to stir things up for some reason, and began buzzing the gathered crowd. Most people grew afraid and scattered, but Amelia stood in the middle of the clearing, transfixed, even when he dove so close to her that she knew "if something went wrong… he, the airplane and I would be rolled up in a ball together." But Amelia didn't care. Something bigger was happening. She said: "I did not understand it at the time but I believe that little red airplane said something to me as it swished by."

World War I ended on November 11, 1918, with the signing of the Armistice, but Amelia remained at Spadina. There was still much work to be done in the hospital. By this time, a deadly worldwide influenza epidemic had reached Canada. The hospitals were overloaded with patients and the death rate was climbing rapidly. Amelia could have chosen to leave at any time, moving to an area that was not afflicted by the

ARMISTICE

An armistice is an agreement to stop fighting.

flu. But she didn't. She stayed where she was needed, working on the wards. By January, she too got sick and developed a sinus infection that required surgery. This was to be the first of several surgeries she would undergo throughout her life for sinusitis—a minor problem with today's antibiotics, but a serious condition at the time.

Amelia went to recuperate at her sister's in February. Muriel was now living in Northampton, Massachusetts, preparing to attend Smith College. To Muriel's delight, Amelia seemed to enjoy taking some time to slow down, although it is probable that she grew restless as time went on. Still, Amelia went for walks with Muriel and even learned a few new skills. She had always had a knack for music and when she saw a banjo in a shop window, she bought it and learned to play. She also took a class intended for female ambulance drivers that included the basics of auto

When World War I ended, there were massive celebrations, such as this tickertape parade in New York City.

"Whileaway"

Looking from golf links.

At Lake George, Amelia stayed in Pedersen Cottage, which was part of "Whileaway."

repair. This would prove very handy in the years to come.

In the summer, Amelia and Muriel joined their mother at Lake George, New York. Amy was in need of a vacation with her girls, as the work of keeping her marriage together was a continual struggle. Most recently, Edwin had decided he wanted to live in California and he was off finding a house on the West Coast. Amy was uncertain if she wanted to join him there.

At Lake George, Amelia became friendly with a young woman named Margaret Balis. Margaret wanted to be a doctor, which inspired Amelia to start thinking along the same lines. After all, Amelia had been a good nurse, she was smart, and she wanted to do something meaningful with her life. Perhaps being a doctor was the way to go. In true Amelia fashion, she implemented this idea right away, moving to New York City in the fall and enrolling at Columbia University to study medicine. She was 22 years old.

Amelia loaded up on courses, but quickly learned that, although she enjoyed the science of medicine, she did not see herself practicing it. This did not keep her from finding fun for herself—she spent hours exploring the underground tunnels that connected some of the buildings at Columbia, and indulged in one of her favorite pastimes— climbing. Her closest friend there was Louise de Schweinitz, who accompanied her on some of these mischievous adventures.

Amelia (in hat) and pal Louise de Schweinitz, who went on to become a doctor.

On one occasion, they climbed into the lap of an enormous statue in front of the Low Library. They sat in the statue's lap, eating cherries and reading poetry! Even more daring, the two also managed to get themselves out onto the domed roof of the library. A staircase led to this high roof, but it was always kept locked. Somehow, Amelia secured the key. As Louise recalled later, "More than once we climbed the endless steps, and up over the roof on our hands and knees to the very top of the dome." During one of their visits to the roof, Louise revealed that she was thinking about getting married and Amelia expressed how she felt about the whole thing. Amelia told her, "I can think of lots of things worse than never getting married, and one of the worst is being married to a man who tied you down."

Then in May, almost as abruptly as Amelia had decided to attend Columbia, she withdrew. Perhaps it really was because she couldn't see herself as a doctor. This realization also happened to coincide with a letter from her father, urging

the whole family to move to California and live together. Amy decided to join him, for he had stopped drinking and it seemed he was making a real effort to reunite his family even though his girls were already grown. Amelia likely had misgivings about this, but her loyalty and love for her family led her to California. Muriel did not want to leave Smith College, so Amelia went on her own, telling her sister, "I'll see what I can do to keep Mother and Dad together until you finish college, Pidge, but after that I'm going to come back here and live my own life." As it turned out, it was a move that would change her life forever.

Amelia enjoyed a life-long habit of climbing onto roofs! Here, she views London from a hotel roof in 1928.

4

Amelia Learns to Fly

When Amelia got to Los Angeles, she met three young men her parents had taken in as boarders, to help with the rent. One of them was Sam Chapman, a handsome engineer. Amelia and Sam took an instant liking to each other and began spending time together, although Sam would never be able to compete with what was about to become her true love.

California was alive with flight. New airfields were popping up all over, and air shows were in abundance. The movie industry provided opportunities for stunt flyers and the rich

Sam Chapman adored Amelia and wanted to marry her.

and famous were spending money on planes and flying lessons. The excitement—and the danger—were palpable. Plane crashes and deaths were fairly common in the early days of aviation, and the component of risk was part of the fascination. Amelia had already gotten a taste for airplanes in Toronto, but she was about to be bit by the flying bug forever.

In December 1920, Edwin took Amelia to a winter air tournament. A few days later, he arranged for her to go for her very first plane ride with pilot Frank Hawks. In *The Fun of It*, Amelia wrote, "As soon as we left the ground, I knew I myself had to fly.... 'I think I'd like to learn to fly,' I told the family casually that evening, knowing full well I'd die if I didn't."

Captain Frank Hawks took Amelia up for her first plane ride, and set the west-to-east nonstop flying record in 1933.

Soon afterward, Edwin took her to Kinner Field in Los Angeles to find out more about flying lessons. Amelia knew she wanted to learn from a woman pilot, especially since Frank Hawks had been fairly condescending about female flyers—taking an extra male passenger up just in case Amelia got hysterical and wanted to jump out! At Kinner Field, Amelia and Edwin met Neta Snook, a fiery pilot just a year older than Amelia who had been flying solo since 1918. Snook was a skilled flight instructor and was impressed with Amelia's calm, clear determination to fly. Likewise, Snook embodied what Amelia was looking for in a teacher. She wrote to Muriel that Snook could "do everything around a plane that a man can do. I'm lucky that she'll teach me...she is a top-notch flier."

When Edwin found out how expensive lessons were, he said no. The family simply didn't have the money. But Amelia was certain of what she wanted to do with her life now, and

PALPABLE

Palpable means capable of being felt.

31

there was no stopping her. She took a job in the mail room of a telephone company to earn the money to pay back Snook, who had agreed to let her fly on credit. This philosophy of "work to fly" was common among aviators who often worked just enough to pay for their flying. The habit would stick with Amelia for life.

Snook gave Amelia her first lesson on January 3, 1921. The two liked each other right away. Their personalities—and paths up to this point—were quite different. Snook had been in charge of her own life for years, while Amelia had been more in keeping with the traditional role of a young woman of the times, generally asking permission to do things and often abiding by her

Neta Snook (on left) was a good first teacher for Amelia, but they had their differences. Their friendship did not last once Amelia moved back East.

Wing Walkers & Barn Stormers

In the 1920s, aviation was relatively new. Planes were still a novelty and not yet used for public transportation. Fliers were on the lookout for fresh and exciting things to do in an airplane. Air shows became popular, and people would flock to these exhibitions. There were large shows that involved multiple acts and stunts, as well as small spontaneous ones often sparked by a barnstormer—a pilot who would land his plane in an open field (often marked by a barn) and set up shop. These impromptu shows would attract nearby people who had seen or heard the plane come in. Sometimes, the pilot even buzzed down a main street to alert the town. People loved to see what those pilots in their flying machines would do next. One of the most exciting stunts was wing walking. Just as it sounds, this was when a person walked out onto the wing of a plane while in flight! Some pilots even performed the harrowing plane-to-plane transfer, climbing from the wing of one plane onto a second plane hovering as close to the first one as possible. Dives, free falls, and dramatic stalls were common ways to thrill onlookers below, too. In addition to performing for the crowds, pilots often took passengers for rides for a small fee. It was a great way for pilots to fund their love of flying and it helped introduce the nation to the joys of flight.

33

parent's wishes—at least, she tried! Snook's example may have been the turning point for Amelia, as she began to follow her own dreams more voraciously from this time on.

The two also shared several important things in common, such as having fathers who had allowed them to play "boyish" games when they were children. Both were intelligent women who had gone to college, and both were from the Midwest. Soon, Snook and Amelia began spending time together off the airfield as well. They even double dated. Amelia was still seeing Sam Chapman, but not exclusively.

At this point, Amelia was already dressing the part of a pilot, wearing long pants, high-laced boots,

The ever-playful Amelia (second from left) and a few friends try out the recently invented pogo stick!

and a leather coat almost down to her knees. But while many female pilots had short haircuts, Amelia's was still fairly long and flowing—even though she had been snipping it bit by bit in secret. It is not clear whether she didn't want to upset her mother by

The "Canuck" in which Snook taught Amelia to fly was a variant of the Curtiss "Jenny" shown here.

cutting her hair, or whether, as she wrote, "I had not bobbed it lest people think me eccentric." It was seen as eccentric enough to simply be a female pilot in the twenties. She eventually changed her mind, however, after a little girl that she met complained Amelia didn't quite look like a pilot with her long hair. The tousled curls she wore from then on would be her signature hairstyle.

From the time of her first lesson, Snook thought Amelia was a "natural." Snook's plane had two open cockpits. A rudder bar and a stick controlled the plane. Much like a steering wheel, the rudder bar, which was moved by foot, turned the plane. The stick, which was worked by hand, took the nose of the plane up or down. Pulling back on the stick made the nose go up, and caused the plane to climb. Pushing forward made the plane dive.

ECCENTRIC
If something is eccentric, it is odd or peculiar.

Snook sat in the rear cockpit; Amelia in the front. Whatever one pilot did with her rudder and stick

was automatically mimicked by the controls in the other cockpit. It was a simple plane with no brakes, no gas gauge, and a tail that dragged on the ground and helped the plane slow down after landing. For her first lesson, Amelia learned how to work the controls and taxi on the airstrip. Next, they went up. Snook was impressed with Amelia's knack for it later saying, "There wasn't much for me to do, she just seemed to take over and do it." Snook, though, was quickly concerned about what she saw as Amelia's recklessness. There were two high tension wires at Kinner Field that needed to be cleared on landing—Amelia preferred to zip between them.

One day, Amelia showed up with money for a rental car and said to Snook, "This is the day I learn how to drive a car.… You rent it, because you have a license, then I'll drive it." The Model T Ford they rented stalled many times while Amelia got the hang of it, and she jumped out each time and cranked it back up. By the end of the day, she could manage well enough.

The Model-T Ford is the type of car in which Amelia learned to drive.

It was around this time that Snook

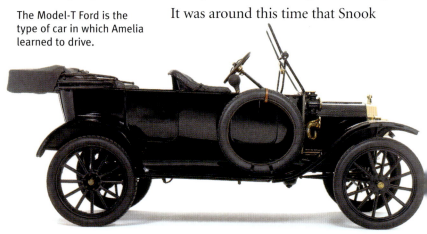

Female Flight Firsts

In addition to the "firsts" that Amelia would achieve, other women broke barriers in the aviation world. In 1910, Blanche Scott took her plane into the air during what was supposed to be a solo ground lesson, making her the first American female pilot. Two years later, Scott's tricks marked her as the first female stunt flier. In 1911, Harriet Quimby became the first woman to get a pilot's license. She was also the first woman to fly the English Channel. In 1921, Bessie Coleman became the first African-American person— male or female— licensed as an aviator. In 1934, Helen Richey was the first woman licensed to fly a commercial airplane. By 1930, there were almost 200 female pilots. Just five years later, there were nearly 800! Today, there are more than 35,000—which is only six percent of the licensed pilots in the United States.

Blanche Scott

Harriet Quimby

and her boyfriend, William Southern, became more serious about each other. When Snook asked Amelia what she thought of him, Amelia replied, "I think he has the mating instinct.…Are you sure you're ready to give up your career?" It was an opinion similar to the one she had shared with her friend Louise back at Columbia. Although she felt comfortable discussing her unconventional ideas about women with people close to her, she kept them to herself in public. They were ideas to which she would remain true.

chapter 5

An Aviator Is Born

Amelia looked every inch the aviator now, and took some pains to do so—staining her leather coat with oil and sleeping in it to give it that well-worn touch. Her appearance made a statement about who she was. She was part of the in crowd at the increasingly popular airfields and wanted the approval of her peers. While Snook donned dirty overalls and often had grease on her face, Amelia strove to be stylish. Her breeches were well-fitted to her body and even with her helmet and goggles on she "looked thoroughly feminine," according to pilot Waldo Waterman.

Since her first day in Snook's plane, Amelia craved her own. She never liked Snook's clunky Canuck. Now Amelia had her sights set on a new plane that experienced designer Bert Kinner had developed. The Airster was small, lightweight, and fun to fly, but Snook and other pilots thought it was

Amelia is decked out in flight jacket and helmet, goggles in hand.

unstable and found the engine unreliable. Amelia didn't care. It was built for speed, ease of maneuverability—and it was pretty. The air-cooled engine made it a simpler plane to maintain, and it was so light she could move it around on the ground by its tail without anyone's help. One historian made the comparison that the Airster was like a swallow and the Canuck, a turkey. Snook remained concerned by her friend's apparent lack of judgment.

This photo appeared on Amelia's pilot's license.

It was clear to her that the Airster was "not a plane for a beginner" and Snook had plenty of evidence that Amelia was just that.

Amelia had been training with Snook for about six months, but in Snook's opinion, she was still making simple mistakes. On one trip Snook described, Amelia changed their intended destination midflight, setting her sights on a much longer trip. When Snook realized where Amelia was heading she asked about the fuel status. Amelia had simply assumed that Kinner had filled the plane and had not checked it herself. Hearing this, Snook took over, turning the plane around and heading back to the airfield. A nervous Kinner was waiting for them, knowing he had not,

in fact, fueled the plane that day.

No matter what Snook may have thought, Amelia's confidence was intact. She felt ready for her own plane and was determined to get it. Of course, she couldn't afford it and Edwin wouldn't buy it for her. So in addition to her work at the telephone company, Amelia took an extra job hauling gravel with a truck. And after much convincing, she also got her mother to contribute some money. In the meantime, Kinner allowed Amelia to use the plane in exchange for him being able to use it for demonstrations whenever he needed to. The plane was hers by her 24th birthday, in 1921. Amelia named her yellow plane the Canary.

By this time, Amelia had logged more than eight hours of time in the air. Snook felt she was ready to solo, but Amelia avoided it. This surprised Snook, who began to suspect that Amelia might have

Amelia's mother said she treated her new plane "like a favorite pony. We said goodnight to it and patted its nose..."

doubts about her own capability. The two had had a few minor crashes. Regarding one of them, in their respective books written years later, they each cast fault on the other. But doubt of her skills was not Amelia's reason for procrastination. While Snook was never one to take chances, Amelia believed experimentation was the road to safety. In her book *20 Hrs., 40 min.*, she later explained her hesitation to solo with Snook: "I refused to fly alone until I knew some stunting. It seemed foolhardy to try to go up alone without the ability to recognize and recover quickly from any position...."

John Montijo, Amelia's second instructor, said she handled her first solo flight "like a veteran."

Snook sold her plane in the fall of 1921 and Amelia found another instructor to continue her training. She chose John "Monte" Montijo, an ex-army pilot accomplished in stunt flying, or aerobatics. "I was then introduced to aerobatics and felt not a bit afraid when sent 'upstairs' alone for the first time," Amelia wrote. Indeed, this first solo flight took place before the year was out. Unfortunately, a shock absorber broke off and she had to end the flight quickly. But it was repaired right away, and afterward she flew to 5,000 feet (1,524 m). Her sister was home for a visit and was happy to witness Amelia's achievement.

Hollywood Heights

As aeronautical acrobatics caught on, Hollywood took notice. They offered everything Hollywood could want—daring adventure, cliffhanger suspense, death-defying stunts. Of course, not all of the stunts did defy death. There was nothing safe about aerobatics and plenty of stunt pilots lost their lives. Still, the movies did wonders for the aviation business, as they brought the glamour of flying to a much larger audience than ever before. One stunt pilot star was Ormer Locklear (shown above). He invented a move called "the transfer," in which a pilot changed from one plane to another in midair, and performed it in movies such as *The Great Air Robbery* and *The Skywayman*.

A female flier, Pancho Barnes—who broke Amelia's speed record in 1930—was a stunt pilot in several films. She also helped found the Motion Pictures Pilots' Association in 1931, dedicated to making sure the pilots risking their lives were well-paid, which wasn't always the case. Amelia's friend Paul Mantz was president of the organization, and was well known for flying a biplane through an open air hangar. Mantz was also instrumental in making it possible to film combat scenes in the air.

Films such as *Wings, Stranger than Fiction, Hell's Angels,* and *It's a Mad, Mad, Mad, Mad World* secured a permanent place for fliers on the silver screen, and stunt flying remains a part of the movie industry to this day.

Amelia soon began flying the Canary in air shows, many of which were by invitation only. She was a desired commodity from the start; people wanted to come out and see her perform. She flew in the Pacific Coast Ladies' Derby with another female pilot, movie star Aloysia McLintic. Amelia didn't much care for exhibition flying, but she knew it was a necessary part of the deal and a good way to earn money to pay for her flying habit. She later wrote: "The minute I flew up to the field I began to feel like a clown, although happily there were two of us female freaks to divide the honors and the odium."

Amelia was already advertising Bert Kinner's Airster in person, by flying it in shows and taking passengers for rides. She became so popular he started featuring her in the magazine ads he ran for his company as well, with titles such as "A Lady's Plane as well as a Man's."

In August 1922, Amelia was the

Amelia stands by her plane after her first solo flight.

topic of a story in the *Los Angeles Examiner*. She had been thinking of heading back East, and the author of the piece

daydreamed about Amelia landing on the campus of Vassar College in a "thrill of thrills." They also ran a photo of Amelia standing by an Airster. The publicity was good for her, but Amelia decided she wasn't yet ready to leave the West Coast. She was enjoying herself. She loved having her sister in town, and the two of them would pack a basket of sandwiches on the weekend and walk out to the airfield to hang out with the pilots. Amelia wrote of this time: "I lingered on in California, another sunkist victim of inertia."

In October 1922, Amelia gave

Air shows like this one were quite popular in the 1920s. One trick was mid-air refueling, in which a wing walker would strap a small gas tank to his back and fill the plane's tank in mid-air!

Ruth Nichols (1901–1960)

Ruth Nichols was a friend of Amelia's and an accomplished pilot. In 1931, Nichols planned a trip to cross the Atlantic, but she crashed in New Brunswick, Canada. The broken vertebrae in her back did not keep her grounded for long. She was soon back in the air, even though she had to wear a steel brace. In 1932, Nichols held three records at the same time—for women's altitude, speed, and women's distance, with a nonstop flight from Oakland, California to Louisville, Kentucky. That same year she became the first woman to fly a regularly scheduled commercial plane.

Muriel and Edwin two tickets to an air show, telling them she would not be able to sit with them. It was a calculated move that would become a habit. If she was going to attempt something in the air, she didn't like having it announced until after she achieved it. Perhaps this was to spare her family and friends from worry, since they were often present to watch her fly. Or perhaps it was to prevent people from trying to talk her out of it. In any case, on that Fall day, Amelia set an altitude record for women by climbing to 14,000 feet (4,267 m) in her Canary.

A few weeks later, pilot Ruth Nichols broke Amelia's record. Naturally, Amelia set out to best it. This time, weather was not on her side. As she reached 10,000 feet

(3,048 m), thick clouds completely obstructed her view. "It was extraordinarily confusing and, realizing I could not go farther, I kicked the ship into a tail spin and came down to 3,000 feet [914 m] where I emerged from the fog and landed," Amelia wrote. It is impossible to know for certain whether she actually did this intentionally, or whether the plane simply went into a tail spin on its own—something she would not have been quick to admit.

Another milestone occurred on May 16, 1923, when Amelia was granted a pilot's license from the Federation Aeronautique Internationale (FAI), the international aviation organization. (The FAI had recently reorganized as the

Amelia's first crash, in 1921, landed her in this cabbage patch.

National Aeronautic Association, including women in its membership—a noteworthy step forward for the times.) Amelia was the 16th woman in the world to receive a license from the FAI/NAA. The document was not required in order to fly, but a pilot did

Amelia's transport license qualified her to carry paying passengers.

need a license if she intended to try and break any official records in the future. Naturally, Amelia wanted this license!

chapter **6**

Another New Start

By spring of 1924, try as they had to stay together, Amy and Edwin Earhart's marriage was still not working. Divorce was an unusual occurrence at the time, but the couple took that final measure and split up for good.

The family finances were in a mess again, too. Amy had already used up most of her inheritance for her daughters' schooling and other expenses, including the Airster. In an attempt to make up some losses, what little was left of the family fortune was invested in a trucking venture. Unfor-

Amelia took this self-portrait while dabbling in photography.

tunately, the investment turned out badly and they lost their money. Amelia felt guilty, as it had been her idea. Muriel had already had to drop out of Smith, and was teaching fourth grade in California. Amelia was working at all sorts of odd jobs in order to make ends meet. She also studied photography at one point, and managed to sell a few of her photographs. One job offer could have been particularly lucrative, but Amelia had the good sense—and the scruples—to turn it down. She was approached by a man who wanted her to fly to Mexico and smuggle liquor out, saying, "A woman can get by where a man can't. No one would ever suspect you."

Although Amelia's romantic life suited her just fine, it is unlikely that Sam Chapman was as content. They were still dating and it seems Amelia was serious about him, but she had no desire to settle down and take up a traditional life. When Sam proposed, she *may* have accepted—

Amelia's mother sometimes worried about her daughter but admired her bravery.

that much is unclear—but they did not make any plans to get married. Meanwhile, her sinus condition had returned and she was in pain. Between their parents' breakup, the family financial situation, and Amelia's own physical state, Amelia and Muriel decided the time had finally come to head back East where they belonged, and leave California behind.

Amelia's sinus condition, for which she had to have another surgical procedure, made it too painful for her to fly across the country. Instead, she sold her plane and bought a car. Did she buy an inexpensive, sensible car? No. She bought a bright yellow Kissel convertible, and nicknamed it the Yellow Peril. If Amelia was going to drive all the way to Boston, she wanted to go in style, and cheer up her mother—who was moving with them—along the way. Muriel went on ahead, by train. She wanted to get back quickly to enroll in summer classes at Harvard. Amelia and Amy, however, would take a long and

This is Amelia's "Yellow Peril." A sculptured likeness of her sits in the driver's seat.

winding scenic route, a surprise Amelia told her mother about as they prepared to leave. Amy's first clue may have been that they began to head north, instead of east.

"Neither she nor I had ever seen some of our best national parks, so I had determined to do some touring," Amelia wrote in *The Fun of It*. A quick glance at a map will tell you that most of the destinations Amelia chose were not on the way to Massachusetts,

Crystal-clear Crater Lake was one of the stops on Amelia and Amy Earhart's cross-country trip.

but Amelia didn't mind. She wanted an adventure. From Los Angeles, their first stop was Sequoia National Park, near Fresno, California. Amelia then drove further northeast to reach Yosemite, in the Sierra Nevada mountains. Then it was on to Crater Lake, in Oregon. At 1,958 feet (597 m) deep, this is the deepest lake in the United States—and the seventh deepest in the world.

Amelia still had more to see, and drove further north into Banff, Canada, then back into the United States to Yellowstone National Park. It was fairly uncommon to travel such distances by car at that time. Between the brightness of their car, and the tourism stickers they picked up everywhere they went, the Earhart women in their Yellow Peril attracted attention. All told, they had turned a possible 3,000-mile (4,828 km) trip into 7,000 miles (11,265 km) and took six weeks to reach

Boston. By the end of the trip, Amelia was in considerable pain, as the operation she had had in California had not done the trick. She braced herself for yet another one, which was performed at Massachusetts General Hospital just three days after their arrival in Boston.

Recovering from her operation took longer than she had hoped, and Amelia stayed in Boston for a few months. With little money, she finally headed on to New York, in order to resume studies at Columbia. She only enrolled for two classes, possibly because that was all she could afford. Amelia was struggling to get by—although, as always, she kept her complaints mainly to herself. Even her close friends didn't find out until years later that Amelia's parents had gotten divorced and the family was having financial troubles. Refusing to ask for help from anyone, she eventually had to withdraw from Columbia and went back to Boston to move in with Muriel and Amy the following May.

The Earhart women lived in this Medford, Massachusetts, house together.

Finding work she liked to do was proving difficult. Flying opportunities were not presenting themselves. She taught English to foreign students at

Harvard and worked in a mental hospital, but did not continue with either. It would have been common for a

woman in her twenties to fall back on marriage at this point. When Amelia had decided to move back to the East, Sam Chapman had followed suit and gotten a job at the Edison Electric Company in Boston. Once she returned to Boston from New York, Sam pressed for marriage again. But Amelia still had no desire for it. Although she was 27, she was not concerned about her future, or the fact that she had tried her hand at so many different jobs. She later wrote: "Experiment! Meet new people. That's better than any college education.... By adventuring about, you become accustomed to the unexpected. The unexpected then becomes what it really is… the inevitable."

She soon discovered an inevitable, it seemed, after applying for a job as a social worker at a settlement house. Social work was a career in which many intelligent women of the time were welcomed. They were able to have authority in their jobs, a rare thing in the 1920s. Amelia was talented at this work and enjoyed it. Denison House was one of the oldest settlement houses in America, started two years after Jane Addams opened Hull House in Chicago. Amelia was following in some powerful footsteps, and she felt it. Other than flying, it was the calling she had been looking for. At Denison House, her intellect and her heart were put to good use.

Amelia thrived at Denison. In her Yellow Peril, she took children to and from the hospital to receive medical care. She set up a mother's club for the Syrian women with small children. She was in charge of escorting one blind little boy to the Perkins Institute for the Blind, and took over care of the kindergarten. The children loved her. She worked there five days a week. She started a club for the Chinese girls, English classes for the Chinese mothers, and helped get a basketball team together. "To me," she said, "one of the biggest jobs of the social worker is to give boys and girls the experiences that will keep them young." Before long, she was living at Denison House full time, and taking her meals with the other resident workers. The move may well have upset Sam, who was patiently biding his time, waiting for her to be ready for marriage and a home of her own. But at that time, Denison was the home Amelia chose.

As busy as she was, Amelia had not given up her passion for flying. In fact, with a regular income from her job, she was able to pursue it again. She met some

Jane Addams was a pioneering social worker and the first American woman to receive the Nobel Peace Prize.

Here, Amelia is surrounded by kids at her beloved Denison House.

local pilots and joined the Boston section of the National Aeronautic Association (NAA). On at least one occasion, she even got to combine her two interests. Traveling as a passenger, she flew over Boston distributing flyers for a fund-raiser for Denison House. The press covered it in the papers the next day.

Around this time, a welcome opportunity presented itself. A Boston architect named Harold T. Dennison (no relation to Denison House) met Bert Kinner, who got him fired up about building an airport in Boston and selling Kinner airplanes. Dennison did just that, and followed Kinner's suggestions to get in touch with Amelia. Amelia invested in the new airport (which opened on July 2, 1927) and became one of the directors—and the only woman on the flying staff. She was also Kinner's East Coast sales representative. Her involvement caught the attention of the press, and Amelia was back in the headlines.

chapter 7

Lady Lindy

In the spring of 1927, someone else was in the headlines—internationally. That someone was Charles Lindbergh, who made the first solo nonstop crossing of the Atlantic in an airplane. He became an instant celebrity of the greatest magnitude, and opened the door for a whole string of "firsts" in the field of aviation. Someone would be the first woman to accomplish this crossing. Might it be Amelia? Five had already failed—and three of them had died trying.

In April 1928, a phone call interrupted Amelia's work at Denison House. She asked the caller if it was important; she did not want to be disturbed while working with the kids. She was assured it was urgent. On the other end, the caller identified himself as Captain Hilton Railey and asked if she was

Lindbergh's plane, the *Spirit of St. Louis*, hangs in the National Air and Space Museum in Washington, D.C.

Charles Lindbergh (1902–1974)

Charles Lindbergh marked the beginning of the celebrity age. Never before had a person become so famous, so fast. He was 25 years old when his nonstop solo flight from New York to Paris made history, on May 20-21, 1927. Following this landmark event, Lindbergh toured the United States—and was mobbed everywhere he went. His single-engine airplane was called the *Spirit of St. Louis* and the tall, handsome pilot with the silver plane quickly went from man to myth. People wanted to know everything about him, much in the same way that some people today track the everyday lives of movie stars and other celebrities.

Lindbergh used his popularity to further the field of aviation throughout his life. Countless pilots were influenced by his accomplishments. He also became known for his opposition to U.S. involvement in World War II, taking the stand that it was a European conflict and America should stay out of it. Some of his comments around this issue implied that Lindbergh was anti-Jewish, and many people were angered. Although controversial, Lindbergh holds an important place in history.

"interested in doing something for aviation which might be hazardous." Once Amelia was satisfied that he was serious, she agreed to meet him in his office that night. He came right to the point, once again. "Would you fly the Atlantic?" he asked. She would—but needed to know more.

It turned out that a man named G.P. Putnam was behind the phone call from Railey. Putnam was a publisher who had handled the publicity of the Lindbergh flight. A bit of a tug-of-war had been going on behind the scenes regarding the first woman's crossing. The flamboyant and wealthy Mabel Boll had made it her goal to be the first female passenger to make the trip across the Atlantic. She claimed to have an arrangement to buy Commander Richard E. Byrd's plane, the *Friendship*, and have it piloted by Wilmer Stultz. Meanwhile, Amy Phipps Guest, who for some reason was irked by Boll's flashy style, secured

Mabel Boll's nickname was the Queen of Diamonds because she wore so many jewels.

both the plane and the pilot right out from under her. The stately and accomplished Guest had set *her* eye on the prize.

Putnam was prepared to manage Guest's flight when her family got wind of her risky plan and ultimately convinced her not to do it. But she didn't back down completely. Guest still had rights to the plane, and did not want to see Boll achieving fame when, in her opinion, there was a worthier female to be found who would represent their sex with distinction. Putnam was asked to find that person. His friend Railey had heard about Amelia Earhart. When Railey interviewed her, he believed he had found the woman they were looking for.

One of the things that struck Railey as soon as he met Amelia was her resemblance to Charles Lindbergh. Many people would go on to make that same comparison, and the nickname Lady Lindy followed her for years. Some believe a photographer deliberately composed certain photos of her to look like Lindbergh and create the illusion. But when Lindbergh's wife Anne met Amelia, she recognized a significant similarity between the two: "It startles me how much alike they are....C. doesn't realize it,...She has the clarity of mind, impersonal eye, coolness of temperament, balance of a scientist."

After passing muster with Railey, Amelia was scheduled for an interview in New York with Putnam. Railey instructed her to keep the meeting a secret. Only Marion Perkins at Denison House was trusted with the information.

She gave Amelia time off and a promise to keep her confidence. (By this time, Amelia was an invaluable part of Denison, and had been made one of its directors.) Once in New York, Amelia met first with Putnam, who then introduced her to two other men who had to approve of her. She impressed the lot.

After that, Amelia was filled in on the details. The pilot, also a skilled radio operator, was Stultz. The mechanic, Lou Gordon. Amelia was asked if she minded that the men would be paid, while she would not. She said she didn't mind; she understood the magnitude of the opportunity, which was worth more than a paycheck. She also understood the risk, as a total of fourteen people had died attempting the crossing. Amelia went back to Boston, while

G.P. Putnam had made a name for himself by publicizing both Lindbergh's flight and Colonel Byrd's expedition to Antarctica.

Putnam checked into her references to confirm that she was the right woman for the job. Two days later, the offer was made—and accepted. Amelia also learned that once the plane was in the air, she would be in charge.

In preparation, Amelia wrote out her will, and letters to each of her parents, in case anything should happen to her. To her mother she wrote, "Even though I have lost, the adventure was worthwhile. Our family tends to be too secure. My life has really been very happy, and I didn't mind contemplating its end in the midst of it." To her father: "Hooray for the last grand adventure! I wish I had won, but it was worthwhile anyway. You know that. I have no faith we'll meet anywhere again, but I wish we might."

Secrecy was the main priority from the beginning. If word got out, they would have been overwhelmed by the press, which would have impeded their progress. It would also tip off any fliers attempting to beat them to their goal. Amelia took Marion Perkins into her confidence once more, and Marion gave Amelia two weeks off. She also trusted Sam with her news, as well as the location of her will and two critical tasks—both to be done only *after* the *Friendship* was in the air. Sam was to contact her mother and fill her in on Amelia's plans, and also deliver a letter to Muriel. In Muriel's letter Amelia wrote: "I have tried to play for a large stake, and if I succeed all will be well. If I don't, I shall

IMPEDE

To impede is to slow down movement or progress by means of obstacles or hindrances.

be happy to pop off in the midst of such an adventure."

Putnam saw major heroine potential in Amelia. Not only did she have the qualifications as a pilot; she was also attractive, intelligent, daring, and poised. He knew if this flight was successful he would have a major star on his hands. The trick was to be *first*. The sooner the better, too, as attempting transatlantic flights was becoming so in vogue, Putnam feared the public would soon tire of it. The race was on.

The *Friendship* was ready in May, but Amelia and the crew had to wait out nearly three weeks of bad weather before they could fly. In the meantime, Amelia had her hands full at Denison House planning summer activities. She also had the chance to get to know the explorer Commander Richard E. Byrd and his wife, who were busy making plans for his next Antarctic expedition. (Byrd was famous for his first 1928–1930 trip there.) Amelia was making great strides in the flying community, as well. She wrote a letter to the National

Commander Byrd posed for this portrait in his expedition garb. He made a total of five exploratory trips to Antarctica.

When Amelia first saw the *Friendship*, it still had wheels. Byrd had the pontoons put on the plane as an added safety measure for over-water flights.

Aeronautic Association, urging them to make more of a place for women in their organization. Their response seems to have been naming her the first female officer of the Boston NAA. In the meantime, she was corresponding with Ruth Nichols about creating a flying organization just for women.

When word came that the weather had cleared and the *Friendship* was ready to go, Amelia went. They had already had two false starts, but this one would be the keeper. In the early morning hours, a tugboat ferried the crew through Boston Harbor and out to the *Friendship*, outfitted with pontoons and bobbing on the waves. They were off!

PONTOONS

Pontoons are attached to a plane instead of wheels, so it can land on water.

chapter 8

"I Was Just Baggage"

O n Sunday, June 3, 1928, Amelia carried with her only the bare necessities, along with a camera, a wristwatch, and a copy of Commander Byrd's book *Skyward.* She wore her usual flying outfit and took no extra clothes, save a fur-lined flight suit for cold weather. The cabin was stuffed with extra fuel tanks so there was just a small space for her to sit. The *Friendship* was a trimotor plane with a wingspan of 71 feet (22 m). Its exterior was a bright orange and gold, making it easier to spot should the crew have to make an emergency water landing. It had stellar radio and emergency equipment. In fact, the plane was so well equipped it was significantly heavier than the one Lindbergh had flown across the Atlantic.

While Lindbergh had made lack of weight a top priority, Byrd's hand in the *Friendship* preparations made safety a main goal—which carried a lot of extra pounds with it. The pontoons contributed greatly to this problem, cutting down on the plane's range. The lighter the plane, the farther it could travel on less gas. The major advantage to the pontoons was that the plane wouldn't sink if it had to land on the ocean. But there were disadvantages, too. In fact, Amelia knew that getting a seaplane up and off of calm water was tricky "because pontoons stick to water much

as a dime sticks to a wet table." Getting the *Friendship* airborne proved extremely difficult.

Three times, Stultz tried to get the plane off the water, but it was too heavy. Each time, they tried creative solutions—such as reducing the weight by dumping several five-gallon fuel cans and shifting their own weights to different parts of the plane. It was no use. They realized they still needed to lighten the load and made the decision for their standby pilot, Lou Gower, to deplane. He would not be going with them. That worked.

Amelia stands, ready for adventure, in front of the *Friendship*.

On the next try, Stultz was able to gain enough speed to get the nose in the air. They were on their way to Trepassey, Newfoundland, for the first leg of the trip. Within minutes, though, the crew had a close brush with death.

WESTERN UNION

Stultz sent this telegram to Putnam, explaining their delay in Newfoundland.

Somehow, the lock on the cabin door broke—and it sprung open! Gordon quickly tied the door to one of the fuel cans, but it wasn't heavy enough. The door began opening again. Gordon and Amelia had to pull it shut with all their strength, while Gordon secured it to a brace in the cabin. Both fliers had come close to falling out! Fortunately, the rest of the trip to Newfoundland was quiet, although thick fog caused Stultz to land in Halifax instead of Trepassey. In Halifax, Stultz was advised to wait until the next day to continue on. The hard part was keeping Amelia hidden, as Putnam preferred for the news to be spread once they arrived at their final destination. The crew did the best they could, sequestering themselves at a small hotel, but by morning reporters had swarmed the place.

Back in Boston, the press was just as abuzz when they discovered a transatlantic crossing was in progress carrying

Amelia Earhart. Putnam reveled in the headlines, but Amelia's mother and sister were not as wild about Amelia's trip. Sam had not been able to get them the news before they read it for themselves in the papers. Amy was miffed—and she wasn't the only one. When Mabel Boll got wind of the expedition, she was furious. From her perspective, Stultz had promised her a crossing, and there he was, up in the air with Amelia Earhart! She set her mind to securing another plane as fast as possible, in an attempt to get there first.

The crew pressed on to Trepassey after having breakfast in Halifax. While in flight, Amelia wrote in her log book: "A flock of birds rise from the water at our shadow. They resemble in movement and shape the spreading out of the little stars in a sky-rocket." As the *Friendship* landed in Trepassey, men on several small boats tried to be the first to lasso the plane and tow it into the harbor. Amelia called them "maritime cowboys" and laughed. Once on the dock, the crew was greeted with exuberance. Amelia telegraphed her mother to tell her not to worry. Her mother rallied, responding cheerfully: "Wish I were with you. Good luck and cheerio. Love, Mother."

If some spirits were high, Stultz's were not. Victim again to foul weather, the *Friendship* remained stuck in Trepassey for two weeks. Stultz, no stranger to the bottle, began to drink. And there was more trouble afoot. Mabel Boll had made good on her threat to find another plane and make the journey across the Atlantic. While Amelia was holed up

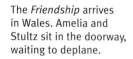

The *Friendship* arrives in Wales. Amelia and Stultz sit in the doorway, waiting to deplane.

in Trepassey, Boll reached Halifax, hot on her heels.

When the weather broke on June 17, it was time to head for England. But there was a problem—Stultz was drunk. Amelia fretted over what to do and decided the only choice was to sober him up fast and stick him in the cockpit so instinct could take over. It may have been brave or it may have been foolish, but in the end it worked. Stultz pulled himself together and they headed for Wales. No doubt Amelia's history with her father's alcohol problem influenced her decision. She did not want to run the risk of her most important adventure being called off. She also didn't want to ruin Stultz's career by requesting another pilot. Amelia believed he would rise to the occasion. Thankfully, he did. En route, the press tracked the *Friendship's* progress closely, taking every chance to remind readers of the dangers involved, capitalizing on the excitement.

Indeed, it was a harrowing trip. The clear weather lasted only about an hour. There was fog, snow flurries, thunder clouds, and strong headwinds. Stultz had to keep changing

68

his flying altitude in an attempt to dodge the various obstacles. Amelia wrote in her log book: "We are bucking a head wind and rain. Heaviest storm I have ever been in, in the air, and had to go through." Stultz radioed in to fix his position, but by morning the radio was not working. For nearly 19 of the 20 hours the crew was in the air, fog made the going rough. Not only that, they were only carrying 700 gallons (2,650 liters) of fuel. If they ran off course and got lost, they would be in trouble. Looking out the window, Amelia couldn't see a thing. When Stultz knew they had been in the air too long without having seen the coast of Ireland, he nosed the plane lower to try and get his bearings. Finally, they spotted land. Not a moment too soon—the *Friendship* was nearly out of gas.

The *Friendship* prepares to leave Burry Port, Wales, en route to Southampton, England.

Gordon was so relieved to see a coastline, he let out a yell and the sandwich he was nibbling at went flying out the window. The crew, however, was still confused as to their location. Amelia logged: "8:50. 2 Boats!!!! Trans steamer. Try to get bearing. Radio won't. One hr's. gas. Mess." They cruised along the coastline, looking for a place to land. Once Stultz selected a spot, he set the *Friendship* down on the water, and the crew tied up to a buoy. There weren't many people around. For an hour, they tried in vain to flag down some help so they could get to shore. Wherever they were, there was certainly no one waiting for them! Finally, a man pulled up alongside the seaplane in a small boat and ferried Stultz ashore so he could call Putnam's agent Captain Railey in Southampton. Meanwhile, people caught wind of what was happening and began to gather.

By the time Railey arrived on the scene, there was a crowd. Railey brought with him reporter Allen Raymond from the *New York Times*, as planned. Excitement escalated. At one point, officials locked arms to form a circle around Amelia

Pilot Wilmer "Bill" Stultz died in July 1929 while doing stunts in his own airplane.

In Trepassey, the crew packed some rations. For the remainder of the flight, Amelia ate only two oranges and six malted milk tablets.

and escorted her into the nearest building. Amelia wrote: "In the enthusiasm of their greeting those hospitable Welsh people nearly tore our clothes off." They had landed not in England, but in Burry Port, Wales—the United Kingdom, nevertheless. They had done it—they had crossed the Atlantic!

Although she expected it, the hype over Amelia was not without its discomfort. After all, she had merely been a passenger. When asked if she was excited, she replied, "I was just baggage, like a sack of potatoes." She made several efforts to focus the press on the pilot and mechanic truly responsible for their accomplishment, to no avail. "I tried to make them realize that all the credit belonged to the boys…it was evident the accident of sex—the fact that I happened to be the first woman to have made the Atlantic flight—made me the chief performer in our particular sideshow." Amelia promised herself she would make the trip again, on her own steam.

71

chapter 9

The High Life

After a night's rest and a refueling of the *Friendship*, Stultz flew his crew, along with Railey and Raymond, to their original destination of Southampton, England. The welcome was wild! Ships blared their horns and the dock was jammed with thousands of well-wishers. Among them front and center was Amy Guest, delighted with the flight's—and Amelia's—success.

Amelia and Amy Phipps Guest in London, June 1928. Amelia is wearing one of the new outfits she bought after landing.

Amelia wrote: "More than ever did I then realize how essentially this was a feminine expedition, originated and financed by a woman, whose wish was to emphasize what her sex stood ready to do."

Also present was the mayor of Southampton, a woman named Foster Welch. The furor of the first 24 hours overwhelmed Amelia. Telegrams, phone calls, and letters all arrived with congratulations—including one from President Calvin Coolidge. There was even one from Mabel Boll, still in Halifax, saying that Amelia had "brought great glory to the American nation." Amelia stayed the night at the Hyde Park Hotel in

The Prince of Wales later became England's King Edward VIII.

London, but found few moments to herself. Guest offered an escape to the privacy of her mansion and Amelia gladly accepted. Guest also took her shopping at Selfridge department store, for Amelia had brought nothing to wear!

Amelia went to all sorts of gala events while in England, and was introduced to luminaries of the time. Alongside Lady Nancy Astor and Winston Churchill, she spoke at a lunch for the Women's Committee of the Air League of the British Empire. She may even have danced with the Prince of Wales. Although at least one historian disputes this, Putnam wrote about it in his biography of Amelia. According to Putnam, the Prince enjoyed Amelia's company very much as "they danced and they danced, and agreed between themselves that fliers were apt to be good dancers." One of her favorite moments was meeting Lady Astor. Amelia was pleased that Lady Astor's focus on her was not founded on her recent trip. "I'm not interested in you a bit because you crossed the Atlantic by air. I want to hear about your settlement work," Lady Astor said.

Bill Stultz, Amelia, and Lou Gordon wave to the crowd welcoming them back to New York.

Before leaving London, Amelia had taken a spin in the small sports plane of Lady Mary Heath, the first British woman to hold a transport license. She liked Lady Heath's Avian so much she made arrangements to buy it, with a loan from Putnam. The Avian was shipped back to the States. Amelia, too, was sent back home, on the luxurious steamship *Roosevelt*.

In New York, the greeting was as big as, if not bigger than, the one in London. By now, Amelia was firmly ensconced in the public mind as a celebrity. They arrived in New York Harbor on July 6 to a spray of fireboats. Then it was on to a tickertape parade, and a luncheon hosted by Commander Byrd. As before, the attention was focused mainly on Amelia, and as before,

ENSCONCED

A person who has settled securely into an activity or role is ensconced in it.

she made every effort to redirect it to the men who had actually piloted the flight. But, nonetheless, she was the main attraction. The group was hailed in Pittsburgh, Chicago, and Boston as well. In Chicago she visited her old high school in Hyde Park, as well as Hull House.

When Amelia got to Boston, she was able to see her family and friends. Familiar faces must have offered a relief alongside the thousands of people who lined the streets as she, Stultz, and Gordon arrived at City Hall. Afterwards, Putnam arrived with Amelia's car, the good old Yellow Peril, so she and her sister Muriel could spend some time alone. Once the parades and benefits were over, Amelia began to work on a book Putnam had asked her to write.

The Chicago Chief of Police pins a star badge on Amelia, in honor of her flight.

It may have been at this time that Amelia realized she was probably not going to be returning to work at Denison. There were too many other things that required her attention just now, although her dedication to Denison House and Marion Perkins likely made her feel a bit torn. She confided to her sister: "I'm afraid my value as a social

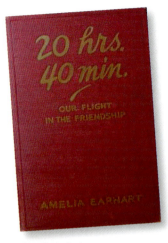

worker is nil while this hullabaloo keeps up." Instead, Amelia accepted Putnam's invitation to seclude herself at his guest house in order to write her book, which she titled *20 Hrs., 40 Min.: Our Flight in the* Friendship. Dorothy, Putnam's wife, got on famously with Amelia. Dorothy admired her, and the feeling was mutual. Amelia even dedicated her book to Dorothy. Whether either of them was aware that Putnam's feelings toward Amelia were changing is unclear, but it did not seem to affect the two women's relationship.

Amelia holed up at the Putnams' home to write her first book.

Putnam, meanwhile, concentrated his efforts on turning Amelia into a bankable star. The book about her flight was only the first step. He and Byrd arranged for Amelia to endorse Lucky Strike cigarettes, the brand Stultz and Gordon had smoked on the trip. This was not Putnam's best decision, as some people were put off by this endorsement, including an editor at *McCall's* magazine, who decided against using Amelia as a contributor. Luckily, Putnam was skilled at what is today referred to as "spin," and used this to interest *Cosmopolitan* magazine in Amelia instead. Soon, she was writing an aviation column for them. Putnam also got her on the lecture circuit, where she talked about the future of air travel and women in aviation.

Amelia took to this lifestyle quite well. She always remained calm and unfettered, an achievement in itself, in light of her

unending schedule of commitments. Sometimes, when fame is thrust upon a person, it throws her off. But Amelia seemed born to handle it. Her newfound popularity was also allowing her to earn some real money for the first time in her life. She was able to pay off debts, live comfortably, and be generous with her funds. A note to her mother implies that this made her happy: "If you know something she [Muriel] wants get it for her and I'll pay. Also you. My treat, at last."

Although she was exceedingly busy, Amelia was also anxious to get back up in the air. Her little Avian had arrived from England and was being assembled at an airfield near the Putnams' house. By the end of August, she was flying again, taking passengers up and giving demonstration flights. Amelia got it in her head that now was the time to take that cross-country flight she had dreamed of in 1924. She took off on August 31, 1928, with a passenger—Putnam. He was not a man who could easily resist an adventure and he seemed to be in as frequent contact with Amelia as possible.

Outside Pittsburgh, Amelia hit a rough patch while landing in a field, and damage was done to the plane. Putnam somehow arranged for the parts to be sent the next day. Amelia then continued on to Los Angeles, where she visited her father. On arriving back in New York she had secured a new record: She was the first woman to make a round-trip flight solo between the coasts. Within a short time, Amelia was what Putnam knew she could be—an American hero. And he may have been her biggest fan.

chapter 10

Races, Records, and Rings

Amelia returned from her cross-country jaunt in October 1928 and wrote about it for *Cosmopolitan*. She also went on an extensive lecture circuit arranged by Putnam. Giving lectures all over the country, to various organizations, was a great way to make money. Just like in her earlier days, she adopted the attitude of working to earn the funds she needed to fly. It was a means to an end, but also gave her the opportunity of writing and speaking about her passion. She enjoyed it, and was good at it. Getting paid for high-profile articles such as "Try Flying Yourself!" or "Why Are Women Afraid to Fly?" was a pretty good deal. In those days, commercial flying was still a huge novelty and publicity was necessary in order to advance the field.

Safety was the main concern for people when it came to aviation. Improvements were frequently made to airplanes to encourage the popularity of commercial flying. Similar to the computers that become quickly obsolete today, airplanes were continually being enhanced and updated. Since the press tended to focus on crashes and disasters, Amelia worked to help promote aviation. Toward this end, in July 1929, Amelia was made assistant to the general traffic manager of Transcontinental Air Transport (TAT), a new airline. She was also given the "special responsibility for attracting women

Here, in July 1929, Amelia is poised to christen TAT's new flagship plane, the Ford Trimotor.

passengers onto the airlines."

Several months earlier, Amelia had decided to go for her commercial transport license. She was sometimes bothered that her reputation was based more on celebrity than skill. Taking the lessons and passing the test for a transport license would certainly advance her skill level. She took the test and became the fourth woman to be awarded this license. In July, Amelia sold her Avian and bought a Lockheed Vega. She needed a more powerful plane

Lockheed Vegas were popular with pilots in the 1920s and 1930s because they were sleek and known for speed. Amelia had hers painted red.

to race in the first cross-country competition for women.

The Women's Cross-Country Air Race was a newsworthy event. On Sunday, August 18, 1929, nineteen female pilots prepared to take off from Clover Field in Santa Monica, California. Will Rogers, humorist and pilot, spoke at the opening of the race. Rogers dubbed it the Powder Puff Derby—a name the women didn't much appreciate but that stuck, nonetheless. Amelia was flying her new Lockheed Vega (the first one had turned out to be such a clunker on inspection that Lockheed had replaced it with a brand new one). The race would begin in California and end in Cleveland.

There were a few accidents in the race and one woman lost her life when her engine failed and her parachute didn't open. Some reporters took this opportunity to call it proof of women's incompetence at flying. The question came up of

whether the race should be stopped, but the pilots voted to continue. Amelia told the press: "It was all the more necessary that we keep on flying." When Amelia had a minor crash and had to fix a propeller, the other contestants waited for her (time down for repairs did not affect the scoring).

This was an appreciated vote of support at a time when some female fliers may have felt prickly about Putnam's involvement in catapulting Amelia's career. Some of them believed his efforts on her behalf worked against them, causing them to lose publicity opportunities while all eyes were on Amelia. Some of them may have also believed her skill level was not equal

Spectators gather to watch the female fliers take off at the start of the Powder Puff Derby.

These are some of the participants in the Women's Cross-Country Air Race in 1929.

to her success. When a person achieves sudden fame, there are often others in her field who will feel overlooked or slighted. It is difficult to know whose perspective is accurate, as everyone sees the world through their own unique set of eyes. However, there were people who felt that Putnam did what he could to hold some fliers back, so Amelia could shine. And they may have been right. Even so, they did not take it out on Amelia. On the second-to-last leg of the race, Amelia came in two minutes ahead of her friend Ruth Nichols. When they took off again, Nichols's plane hit a tractor and flipped over several times. Amelia jumped out of her Vega and rushed to the dismal scene. Amazingly, Nichols was unharmed.

Louise Thaden won the race, with Gladys O'Donnel coming in second. Amelia came in third, "frantically braking and attempting to avoid a ground loop" on a bumpy landing.

But she won the respect of pilot Elinor Smith, who had seen firsthand Amelia's lack of skill at handling a heavy plane just months earlier. "I was filled with admiration for her" wrote Smith, "…and there was absolutely no way she could have built up enough air time to be at ease…this was gut courage that transcended the sanity of reasoning."

Soon after the derby was over, Amelia, Neva Paris, Louise Thaden, and others called a meeting of the female pilots and proposed they form an organization. It was not a new idea; Amelia had first written to Nichols about it in 1927. Now, it seemed the time was right, and the group grew into the world's most prestigious collection of female pilots. Their goal was simple: "to provide a close relationship among women pilots and to unite them in any movement that may be for their benefit or

Elinor Smith (1911–)

Elinor Smith had her first airplane ride when she was only six years old. That might not seem unusual today, but in 1917 airplanes had been around for less than 15 years. She was only 15 when she soloed for the first time, and she became the world's youngest licensed pilot the next year. Elinor set many world records, and at one time sported the nickname "Flying Flapper of Freeport," from her hometown of Freeport, Long Island. Her most famous stunt was flying under all four of New York's East River bridges in 1928. Although Elinor believed Amelia's flying skills could be better, she admired her courage and liked her very much.

The Ninety-Nines

The Ninety-Nines is an international organization of female pilots started by a group of women, including Amelia, in November 1929. They are still going strong today, with more than 6,000 members all over the world. The Ninety-Nines are dedicated to archiving the history of women in aviation, and their museum houses a vast collection of oral histories, memorabilia, and biographical information. Since the beginning, the Ninety-Nines have always worked to bring women fliers together and increase job opportunities. They also provide scholarships for aviation education. In 2001, the Ninety-Nines were inducted into the Oklahoma Air Space Museum Hall of Fame.

for that of aviation in general." There was some debate over what to call the organization. In the end, Amelia suggested naming it after the number of original members. When ninety-nine fliers signed up, they had their name. Two years later, the Ninety-Nines elected Amelia as their president.

With the race behind her, Amelia spent some time in California before moving back to New York. This gave her a

chance to see old friends and visit her father, who had since remarried a woman named Helen. Edwin was not well and Amelia wrote back to Muriel: "He looks thinner than I've ever seen him, and Helen says he has no appetite at all and tires very quickly now." Although she had been fairly independent from her family's needs for a while, this was a time when Amelia felt responsible for their well-being once again. Not only was her father ill and financially insecure, her sister was having marriage troubles, and Amy had never really taken charge as the head of the family. Amelia seemed to take the job in stride, and paid off her father's mortgage.

Once Amelia returned to New York, she wanted a place of her own. She was still busy on a packed lecture circuit for Putnam, and often took long flights for business, staying with friends as she was apt to do. But she needed a spot to call home. In the 1920s, a single woman could not live just anywhere. Hotels were out of the question and she didn't want to take a room in a boarding house. A solution came about when the American Woman's Association (AWA) opened a women's club in Manhattan, complete with residences. It was perfect.

The beautiful new building boasted a pool, gymnasium, library, dining room, roof garden, and an auditorium. It was

A portrait of Edwin Earhart, taken in 1930 in California.

Amelia sits on the beach between G.P. Putnam's son, David, and wife, Dorothy.

even walking distance from *Cosmopolitan*. Amelia moved in, along with her secretary, Nora Alstulund, who helped her keep up with her ever-mounting correspondence and scheduling.

In December 1929, Dorothy and Putnam's marriage fell apart. Some believe it had been in trouble for a while, having nothing to do with Amelia. Others believe it was because Putnam was in love with his star flier. The truth probably lies somewhere in the middle.

The Putnams divorced and Dorothy moved to Florida. Putnam proposed to Amelia several times, but she kept saying no. She was still not a big subscriber to the idea of marriage. In fact, Amelia had seen Sam back in November 1928. It seems the two discussed their relationship because on November 23. Amelia announced to the press: "I am no longer engaged to marry." She and Sam stayed close friends for the rest of her life, and Putnam's proposals did not seem to change Amelia's mind about marriage.

She was also single-minded when it came to setting records. She claimed several in 1930. On June 25, Amelia set two women's speed records in her Vega. The first was for a 100-kilometer run with no load, clocking 174.89 miles (281.46 km) per hour. The second was for carrying a load of 500 kilograms the same distance, with a speed of 171.49 mph (275.99 kph). On July 5, she set another, traveling a 3-kilometer course at 181.18 mph (291.58 kph).

Around this time, Amelia would fly to visit her father, whose health was rapidly declining. Edwin Earhart died of stomach cancer on September 23, 1930. Shortly thereafter, Putnam proposed one more time. This time, Amelia agreed. They married quietly in Connecticut in February 1931. The night before the wedding, however, Amelia wrote Putnam a letter on her continued doubts about marriage in general, told him she would need plenty of time to herself, and asked him to let her go if things didn't work out within a year. He agreed.

The newly married couple, Amelia and G.P. Putnam, pose for a photograph.

11
The Fun Of It

Amelia's taste for setting records and Putnam's desire to keep her in the press were a perfect match. When they weren't working, the couple did find time to enjoy their surroundings in Rye, New York. Amelia seemed to like domestic life some of the time. She asked her mother to send a few family items for her home, such as a table, silverware, candlesticks, and books. "I should like the old quilts etc.," she wrote, "and the things which were Grandma's." Amelia also enjoyed planting in the garden.

Amelia later dabbled in other talents, such as designing clothes. She started by designing a flying uniform for the Ninety-Nines, although the group never ended up agreeing on one suit that everyone liked. From there, Amelia designed tailored

DESIGNED BY
Amelia Earhart

In the early 1930s, Amelia's own line of designer clothes were sold in fancy department stores.

Amelia got the hang of this autogiro in 1931.

clothes for women. The brochure description made a societal comment: "This is an era of feminine activity....Modern women are strenuously active." Amelia had learned to sew her and Muriel's clothes as a girl, when their family was down on their luck. But these new pursuits did not dampen her taste for flying and adventure for a moment. Just a few months after the wedding, Amelia got back to breaking records in the air.

The autogiro has an engine-powered front propeller, like an airplane, as well as a top roter that makes it look somewhat like a helicopter. But, unlike a helicopter, the autogiro's overheard roter blades rotate by air rushing through them instead of by motor. Invented in Spain, the autogiro had recently had its first test flight in Pennsylvania. Amelia wanted to try it out, and Putnam went along for the ride. One day, in April 1931, she tested it dozens of times, getting a feel for the new contraption. Then she took it up for a solo trip—the first time a woman had done so. She even managed to set an altitude record in it, climbing to 18,415 feet (5,613 m). The next day she topped that record with an additional 500 feet (152 m). It wasn't all picture-perfect, though. Amelia had a few accidents in the autogiro that didn't get much press coverage. She attributed the

Amelia and George relax near their home in Rye, New York.

mishaps to her lack of skill.

By 1932, Amelia had finished writing her second book, *The Fun of It: Random Records of My Own Flying and of Women in Aviation.* Amelia was still bothered by the feeling that she had just been "baggage" on her first transatlantic flight. She had always had it in her mind to make the flight solo at some point in the future. That time had come. Her Lockheed Vega was excellent for flying long distances. Adding to the mix was the fact that Elinor Smith was also getting ready to attempt to be the first woman to make the run now nicknamed the Lindbergh Trail.

One morning, over breakfast with Putnam, Amelia posed a question to her husband: "Would you mind if I flew the Atlantic?" Although he recalled feeling "a clutch at the heart," he also said he felt "something akin to elation, in the presence of so adventurous a spirit." Her plane was outfitted and modified for the long flight. Amelia took care to increase her instrument-flying skills, an area in which she'd always needed more work. As with the previous transatlantic flight, Amelia kept her plans secret from anyone who wasn't necessary to the planning. She stayed perfectly calm the entire time.

On the day Amelia got word that her plane was ready and the weather was clear, she hurried home to change into her flying gear and gather minimal belongings. She took a toothbrush, a comb, a thermos, and a can of tomato juice. On her wrist she wore a bracelet her husband had given her that she considered a good luck charm. Amelia was ready to go. The accomplished engineer and flier Bernt Balchen, who had helped her plan the flight, flew Amelia to her departure point in Harbor Grace, Newfoundland. Up-to-date weather reports came in and the final decision to leave was made. From that point on, Amelia was on her own.

On the evening of May 20, 1932, she took off. Five years earlier, to the day, Lindbergh had taken off from New York for his transatlantic flight. Since then, no one else had achieved the flight completely solo.

The first few hours were fine, but then the altimeter failed, which kept Amelia from measuring her altitude for the remainder of the flight. She had more problems about four hours out. The plane took on some ice and went into a spin. "I did my best to do exactly what one should do with a spinning plane and regained flying

This view of the cockpit in Amelia's Lockheed Vega gives a sense of what it felt like to sit there.

control as the warmth of the lower altitude melted the ice," she later wrote. She steadied the plane, too close to the surface of the ocean for comfort, and then flew a bit higher. Once the sun rose, things were easier. She was about two hours from land, though, when she detected a fuel leak. Land couldn't come soon enough. In her personal log, published for the first time in 1997, Amelia wrote: "If anyone finds the wreck know that the non success was caused by my getting lost in a storm for an hour and then the exhaust manifold, resoldered at St. John, burned out and I have crawled near the water for hours dreading fire." Harrowing as the trip was, she did touch down in an Irish field, safe and sound. The long flight took nearly 15 hours, but she was the second person to solo across the Atlantic, and the first woman! She told reporters she hoped her "small exploit

Amelia waves to the crowd greeting her after landing in a field in Culmore, near Londonderry, Northern Ireland, in May 1932.

has drawn attention to the fact that women are flying too." In fact, this flight made her a superstar.

Amelia had landed near Londonderry in Northern Ireland. After calling home and answering reporters' questions, she rested overnight. Then it was on to London, for a warm welcome.

After making calls and collecting telegrams from the post office, Amelia returns to the farmer's cottage near where her plane landed.

Meanwhile, well-wishers sent messages, including Ruth Nichols and Elinor Smith. Nichols wrote: "You beat me to it…but it was a splendid job." Lindbergh himself sent word: "Your flight is a splendid success."

A whirlwind tour of Europe followed, with Putnam meeting Amelia in France. From France, they went to Italy and Belgium before returning to the United States. In Washington, D.C., President Hoover gave Amelia a Special Gold Medal from the National Geographic Society, and the Senate bestowed upon her the Distinguished Flying Cross. She was the first woman to receive this honor.

Amelia showed no signs of slowing down. She pursued more firsts—including a speed record between Los Angeles and Newark in July 1932, which she then topped for the same route in August. Amelia also became a frequent guest of the next U.S. president to take office, Franklin Delano Roosevelt, and his

Amelia and Eleanor Roosevelt on a short plane ride together. Amelia is pointing out the White House to the First Lady.

wife, Eleanor. The two women had become friendly after Eleanor contacted Amelia with congratulations on her transatlantic flight.

In 1933, with Amelia's career in a solid place, Putnam took to pursuing more of his own interests once again. He was hired by Paramount Pictures to come up with ideas for innovative films. Consequently, he and Amelia began to spend more time in California. They rented a house at 10515 Valley Spring Lane, in Hollywood. Amelia's mother came out and stayed with them for a while. And Paul Mantz, a stunt pilot in the movies, became a close friend.

When Amelia set her sights on flying from Hawaii to California, Mantz was there to help. So far, no one had ever flown solo on that route before, a complicated path that spanned more than 2,000 miles (3,219 km). Amelia wanted to do it. She painted her Vega red, and Mantz agreed to be her technical consultant. As before, plans were kept from the press. But when it was found out that her plane would be equipped with a two-way radio intended for communicating with ships while flying over water, suspicions were raised. Curiosity was piqued even further when Putnam, Amelia, Mantz, and his wife set sail for Hawaii in December 1934. The plane was on board,

When Amelia traveled to England in 1932, she forgot her passport. This new one was issued to her during her trip. Note that the year of her birth is incorrect.

covered with a tarp to hide it from view.

On January 11, 1935, Amelia took off from Honolulu and headed to Oakland, California. She radioed in several times, saying that everything was fine. She later wrote: "Stars hung outside my cockpit window near enough to touch." When she arrived to a crowd of more than 10,000 waiting to greet her, Amelia became not only the first *woman* to solo from Hawaii to California, but the first *person*. She was no longer following anyone else's trail; she was blazing her own. Upon hearing the news, her mother told a reporter, "I knew she would do it.… We like to see what a person can do."

Amelia studies her charts in Hawaii, waiting to take off for the mainland.

12

Pushing the Limits

Amelia's confidence was greater than ever. She was still busy giving lectures, corresponding with Amy and Muriel, spending time with Putnam, and seeing her pilot friends when possible. But she was ready for the next adventure. At a dinner in New York, Amelia was invited to make a goodwill flight to Mexico. Mexico's leader, President Lázaro Cárdenas, planned to welcome her on arrival. The Mexican government also offered to issue a commemorative

When Amelia arrived in Mexico City, she was given a traditional Mexican cowboy outfit in beautiful blue and silver.

airmail stamp, the sales of which would help fund the trip. Amelia planned for a nonstop flight between Burbank, California and Mexico City, Mexico.

On April 19, 1935, she set off—and was almost to her destination when she noticed she was slightly off-course. After something flew in her eye and hampered her vision, she decided to land. She discovered she was only about 50 miles (81 km) from her intended destination, and was

annoyed that her nonstop goal was fouled. Amelia took off once again and reached Mexico City shortly, to the applause of a large crowd. Her return flight to New Jersey offered her a second chance to make the trip nonstop, which she did. On arrival in Newark, she was met by a mob and needed a police escort to get off the airfield.

Amelia cared deeply about the equality of women. Before leaving for Mexico she wrote to Putnam: "Women must try to do things, as men have tried. When they fail, their failure must be but a challenge to others." A few years earlier, in a conversation with President Hoover, she had said, "I know from practical experience of the discriminations which confront women when they enter an occupation where men have priority in opportunity, advancement, and

Amelia urged her female students at Purdue to study what they wanted and not get married too soon.

protection." Amelia believed that continuing to press on with her own pursuits in aviation was the best way to prove this was true. In the meantime, she accepted a part-time job at Purdue University, which had a growing aviation department. Amelia counseled female students on their careers.

When people found out Amelia Earhart would be counseling at Purdue in the fall of 1935, twice as many girls enrolled as in the previous year. The school even ran out of dorm space! The university president was grateful, and extremely supportive of Amelia. And what was her next project? Nothing less than a trip around the world, by way of the equator—a 25,000-mile (40,234 km) trip. It was one of the last records left to break at a time when other pilots were vying for press attention with their own record-breaking accomplishments.

Paul Mantz ran a charter service and loved to fly Hollywood celebrities around in his plane.

Although Amelia wanted to open a flying school with her friend Paul Mantz, she also wanted to make one last major flight before taking on that business venture. Through the Purdue Research Foundation, the university helped Amelia buy a Lockheed Electra, outfitted with the state-of-the-art equipment

Amelia and the Boys

Amelia got along well with most male aviators, even though it was a male-dominated field. It may have been her easy manner, which made her confident without seeming arrogant. In fact, despite the fact that many pilots—male and female—did not consider her to be among the most skilled, they admired her courage enough not to begrudge her success. It was a common sight to see Amelia with a group of men at an airfield, discussing the finer points of aviation. Two of her close friends were Wiley Post and Will Rogers. Post was a daring pilot who was the first civilian to fly around the world in 1931, and Rogers had done much to popularize aviation. In 1935, the two set off on a much-talked-about flight to the Arctic Circle. Tragically, their plane crashed in August, about 300 miles from their goal, killing them both.

Wiley Post and Amelia

needed for such a huge undertaking. The plane was registered in her name but belonged equally to the foundation. The plan was for her work to benefit them both. The Electra was ready on her 39th birthday—July 24, 1936.

Amelia asked Mantz to train her in her new double-engine Lockheed, a type of aircraft she had never flown before. She also simply needed more time in the air. In 1935, Amelia had made 136 speeches, which hadn't left much time for flying. She barely had time to visit her sister, who now had two children and a rocky marriage. With family often

on her mind, however, Amelia took the time to plan a surprise for her mother, sending Amy on a trip to Europe in the summer of 1936.

Once Amelia's plane was ready, she and Mantz tested it often. In September 1936, she entered the Bendix Air Race between New York and Los Angeles, to see what the Electra could do. Her friend Helen Richey was her copilot. A large hatch popped open during the flight, and they finished the race in fifth place. Louise Thaden and Blanche Noyes won. A few months later, around New Year's, Thaden went to see Amelia to express her concerns about her friend's round-the-world plans. "It seems to me you've got everything to lose and nothing to gain," she told her.

Amelia flies her Lockheed over the Golden Gate Bridge, en route from Oakland to Hawaii on March 17, 1937.

Amelia was not deterred. In the meantime, Putnam paved the way for securing the necessary permissions to fly over many nations—each country needed to say yes. He wrote to the Bureau of Air Commerce and the secretary of the Navy to get clearances, and made detailed arrangements for accessing weather reports along the way. He assured the authorities the plane would not be carrying weapons or movie cameras. Pre-World War II tensions in the Pacific were mounting. The pair needed to make the fact that they had no ulterior motives clear. Amelia even wrote directly to President Roosevelt: "Like previous flights, I am undertaking this one solely because I want to, and because I feel that women now and then have to do things to show what women can do."

Amelia knew she would need a navigator to succeed at this long and complicated flight around the equator. The trip would require charts and maps of many different countries and precise refueling stops. She chose Harry Manning as her radioman and navigator, and Mantz would make sure the plane was in tip-top shape. Manning was the

Louise Thaden (1905–1979)

A friend and competitor of Amelia's, Louise Thaden was an accomplished pilot and one of the co-founders of the Ninety-Nines. Thaden got her pilot's license in 1927, becoming the first woman in Ohio to receive one. She was also the fourth woman to earn a transport rating. In 1929, Thaden won the Women's Air Derby Race in 1929, as well as the Bendix race in 1936. Amelia competed in both of these competitions.

Mantz, Amelia, and Noonan are greeted in Hawaii with good wishes and plumeria leis.

captain who had ferried her back home after the *Friendship* flight. She also added a second navigator, Fred Noonan. He was an experienced navigator and pilot, but he was also an alcoholic. Amelia had faith in Noonan, and believed his promise to stay sober for the trip.

On February 12, 1937, Amelia announced her plans to the world. The first leg of the trip was made on March 17, from Oakland, California, to Honolulu, Hawaii. (That same day, Pan American Airlines set off with its first Western passengers to the Pacific, traveling a different route.) In addition to Amelia, Mantz, Manning, and Noonan were aboard. Manning would stay in Hawaii and Noonan was only to accompany her as far as Howland Island in the mid-Pacific, the first scheduled stop after Hawaii. The fact that the Electra broke a speed record reaching Honolulu

struck Amelia as "an interesting commentary on the progress of flying equipment," since they had gone "about as slowly as possible."

On March 20, after the plane had been serviced and a malfunctioning propeller fixed, Amelia began to take off from Hawaii. On the way down the runway, one of the wings dipped down and the plane swerved. An attempt to control the plane sent it skidding in a wide circle. Some landing gear broke off and sparks flew. Amelia cut the engine to prevent a fire, but the damage was done. No one was hurt, but the plane needed major repairs and was shipped back to the Lockheed factory in California. The news got worse: It would take five weeks and more than $25,000 to fix the Electra. Amelia and Putnam invested their savings, and borrowed from friends. In the meantime, they waited. Unfortunately, Manning could not afford to wait, as he had to get back to captain his ship. Amelia would be going on without him.

Amelia and others survey the damage just after the crash in Hawaii. A wet runway may have contributed to the plane skidding.

13

That Fatal Flight

While the Electra was being repaired, a few changes were made. Manning had been the one who knew how to use the Morse Code equipment. Without him on board, Amelia decided the plane would be better off without its weight. Likewise, she had the heavy 250-foot (76 m) trailing radio antenna taken off as well, perhaps reducing her ability to send and receive messages in wide expanses of the south-central Pacific. It was a decision that had dire consequences—or didn't. Randall Brink, author of *Lost Star: The Search for Amelia Earhart,* contends the real reason for the antenna's removal was that the Electra was fitted with secret state-of-the-art DF (directional finder) equipment. Other explanations suggest that the antenna was not taken off, simply shortened and improved. This is a good example of how theories vary regarding certain details of Amelia's last flight.

The plane was ready for takeoff in May. Since seasonal weather patterns differ, the delay

Amelia looks on as mechanics work on her plane.

meant Amelia would be more likely to encounter spring storms along her original route heading west around the world "at its waistline." Instead, she changed the plan and reversed the route, heading east. Amelia and Noonan took off from Oakland on May 21, 1937, heading to Miami, where the first transoceanic leg would begin. Putnam and a flight mechanic were also along for the ride. Minor kinks in the system were found during the flight and the Electra was repaired and checked out

George and Amelia share a goodbye in Miami.

during the days spent in Miami. The Pan Am mechanics who worked on the plane were impressed with Amelia. Once again, her attitude and competence elevated the cause of women everywhere. About the mechanics, a reporter wrote: "There was an almost audible clatter of chips falling off skeptical masculine shoulders."

Amelia was excited about her trip, but a comment she made seemed ominous in hindsight: "I have a feeling there is just about one more good flight left in my system and I hope this trip is it." On June 1, after saying goodbye to Putnam, Amelia and Noonan took off from Miami, en route to San Juan, Puerto Rico—heading ever closer to the equator. From there, it was on to Caripito, Venezuela, and then to

July 9, 1937: Amelia and Noonan (far left) have lunch during a stop in Caripito.

Paramaribo, Dutch Guiana (now Suriname).

The trip to Paramaribo was over dense jungle, and Amelia wondered what kind of airfield would be waiting for her there. She was likely relieved to see a beautiful clearing with a bright orange wind sock indicating the direction of the wind. People on the ground were waiting to welcome them with sandwiches and orange juice, and escort Amelia and Noonan on a trip to the colorful marketplace. From Paramaribo, they flew on to Fortaleza, Brazil. On the way there, they crossed the equator for the first time.

In Fortaleza, Amelia and Noonan stayed in the Excelsior Hotel and washed up a bit while the plane was refueled and cleaned. She also took the opportunity to write a letter to Putnam: "For a female to be traveling as I do evidently is a matter of puzzlement to her sheltered sisters hereabout, not to mention the males. I'm stared at in the streets." After two days, they made the short hop to Natal, Brazil.

After leaving Natal, they hit a major rainstorm. "Have never seen such rain. Props a blur in it," she wrote. It took a long 13 hours and 12 minutes to travel 1,900 miles (3,058 km), crossing the Atlantic from South America and arriving in St. Louis, Senegal, on June 7. Amelia had made a slight error in navigation, which is why they hadn't landed at their original target, Dakar, the capital of French West Africa. The next day, they went on to Dakar. They were wined and dined by the governor-general, who put them up in his mansion. The Electra was well taken care of, too. A broken fuel meter was repaired, and the engine was checked. With tornadoes in the forecast, they changed their route to travel a bit north across central Africa, landing gently in the town of Gao. Imagine how exciting it must have been for Amelia to fly over the very places she dreamed about and studied on maps when she was a child!

The trek over Africa was hard because, as Noonan wrote, "the maps of the country are very inaccurate and… misleading." Still, they made it to Fort-Lamy, near Lake Chad, without any problems on June 11. There were many stops along the way, as well as sights to be seen. They even spotted a herd of hippos from the air. At Fort-Lamy, Amelia's interest in social issues was alive and well as she noted, with what might have been amusement, that "killing time appears to be the chief occupation of the males."

The Electra takes off from Caripito, as Amelia and Noonan make their way to Paramaribo.

They saw huge salt dunes near Massawa, and flew along the Gulf of Aden and the Arabian Sea. In Karachi, India, Amelia went for a ride on a camel, Noonan calling after her, "Better wear your parachute!" She also received a call from Putnam there on June 15, and her spirits were clearly up.

Throughout the trip, Amelia's log notes were sent back to the newspapers tracking her progress. The pair left Karachi for Calcutta on June 17. The weather on the way to Calcutta was rough, with strong winds from the monsoon season. On June 18, they tried to make it to Bangkok but only got as far as Rangoon, with a brief stop in Sittwe, due to heavy rains. Then it was on to Singapore and Bandung, crossing the equator for the third time on their way there. In Bandung, on the island of Java, the Electra was

Amelia took some time to see the sights. Here, she is seen sitting on a camel in Karachi.

Workers refuel the Electra in Bandung. Note the words "Earhart's Flight" on the barrels.

serviced and they had a chance to do some sight-seeing. Their excursion even included a trip to see an active volcano! Amelia and Noonan stayed in Bandung until June 27. Accounts vary as to whether Noonan begin drinking while there.

The next destination was Darwin, Australia, with a brief refueling stop on Timor Island, which turned into an overnight stay. Amelia preferred to rest and get a fresh start early the next day. From Darwin, they flew to Lae, New Guinea. There were only two stops left before arriving back in California—Howland Island, and Honolulu, Hawaii.

The task of finding Howland Island, a tiny speck in the Pacific Ocean, had always been the most worrisome part of the trip. The 2-mile (4 km)-long, 1/2-mile (4/5 km)-wide island was situated about halfway between New Guinea and Hawaii. In 1935, the United States was already working on marking the island to use for emergency landing purposes for Pan American airlines, which was starting to research flying

routes in these areas. At the time of Amelia's flight in 1937, a landing strip had recently been completed. Even though two U.S. Coast Guard ships would be on the lookout for her plane, it was an extremely demanding navigational feat to locate and land the Electra on this pinpoint in the middle of the ocean. In the dark, celestial navigation would be necessary. Amelia was lucky to have Noonan, who had experience mapping

Amelia climbs on the Electra's roof upon arrival in Lae, New Guinea. She looks like she's enjoying her adventure!

this part of the world. And although some accounts indicate he may have been drinking in Lae, others refute that idea.

The Electra was loaded down with the 1,100 gallons (4,164

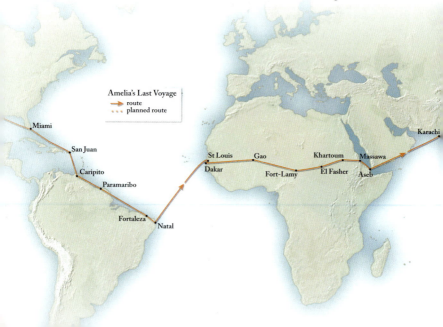

liters) of fuel needed for the long haul—Howland Island was 2,556 miles (4,114 km) from Lae. It was July 2, 1937. Word was sent to the press as soon as they were airborne. Amy Earhart, listening back home on the radio, must have felt relief to get news that her daughter was successful thus far. The ship *Itasca* sat waiting off the coast of Howland. The plan was for Amelia to contact the *Itasca* fifteen minutes before each hour and fifteen minutes after. Updated weather information would be sent to the Electra from the *Itasca*—as well as radio signals that would guide her to Howland.

The night before she left, Amelia thought about how far she had come on the trip, and how far she had to go. She wrote: "…The whole width of the world has passed behind us—except this broad ocean. I shall be glad when we have the hazards of its navigation behind us."

Oakland

Honolulu

Howland Island

twe
Bangkok

Singapore

Surabaya   Lae
3andung   Timor Island
                Darwin

Equator

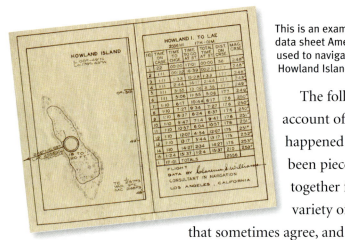

This is an example of a flight data sheet Amelia would have used to navigate between Howland Island and Lae.

The following account of what happened next has been pieced together from a variety of sources that sometimes agree, and sometimes disagree. Harry Balfour, a radio operator at Lae, received a transmission from Amelia about an hour after takeoff. He then attempted to radio her that winds were much stronger than anticipated, but there is no evidence that she received those messages. About four hours into the trip, it is mainly agreed, Balfour did hear a message from Amelia reporting that everything was fine. He later received another similar message from the Electra. Amelia was on course, about 850 miles (1,368 km) out from Lae. It was the last time she would sign off saying that everything was OK.

About four hours from Howland Island, Amelia transmitted a message saying the weather was overcast. Part of the problem with her transmissions seems to have been that there was some confusion about which frequencies the *Itasca* and the Electra should use to communicate with each other. The *Itasca* sent several messages to the Electra, only one of which seems to have been received by Amelia. Making matters

worse, the transmissions Amelia sent indicated that, although she was on course, the headwinds may have been causing her to travel much slower than intended. She was likely running dangerously low on fuel by the time she was within reach of Howland Island.

About 15 hours into the flight, the *Itasca* heard Amelia say "cloudy." An hour later, the ship reported hearing her, but wasn't able to make out what she was saying. After more than 17 hours, the *Itasca* heard this message: "We must be on you but cannot see you but gas is running low—been unable to reach you by radio—we are flying at altitude 1000 feet [1,609 km]." If the Electra truly had been close to the *Itasca*, Amelia and Noonan would have been able to see the cloud of black smoke the ship was sending up as a signal to guide them. Visibility was clear. The Electra, however, seemed to be nowhere in sight.

The last time a transmission was sent, after Amelia had been in the air for more than 20 hours, her voice sounded panicked. It was now two hours past sunrise and the plane had been in the air too long. She radioed in, "We are running north and south." And then, silence. Amelia Earhart was gone.

This is the cockpit of Amelia's Electra.

chapter 14

The Search for Amelia

The *Itasca* waited—hoping—for an hour and a half before sending word that the Electra had not been located. The plane had been equipped with a life raft and survival supplies, in case of a water landing. If Amelia had been able to take the plane down safely, it was within the realm of possibility that the fliers could survive for a while. An extensive search was launched to find the plane and its crew. In the past, Putnam had waited anxiously for Amelia, who had always arrived home safely. This time would be different.

As Putnam paced the coast guard station in San Francisco, awaiting any news, the *Itasca* and other navy ships sailed the waters in range of Howland, and nearby Baker Island. Military planes were also used to scan the area. There was nothing. The search area widened. Still nothing. This was a remote area of the Pacific that was not well-

Amelia made headlines on this Baltimore paper as the world searched for answers about her missing plane.

traveled. And if Amelia hadn't reached Howland or Baker, there was no other land anywhere nearby. The likelihood that Amelia and Noonan had landed on the water and were in grave danger—if they were alive at all—was real. The stakes rose higher with every passing hour, every passing day. Even if the fliers had survived a crash, there were other things to contend with, such as overexposure to the sun and lack of fresh water.

Amelia's tragedy quickly became part of popular culture. Here, a 1939 sheet music cover features a tribute to the lost legend.

On July 6, the Japanese government offered its assistance and two Japanese navy ships aided in the search. It seems unlikely that the Japanese, as some rumors later claimed, would have captured Amelia had they found her. Throughout this time, false radio signals and false hopes were frequent. Seasonal storms made things even more difficult. As the days passed, hope faded. Putnam returned home to wait things out there. On July 20, the *New York Times* printed a farewell to Amelia.

Time continued to pass without any good news. Sadly, Putnam received several fake tips about his missing wife, many of them from people looking to cash in on the tragedy after they heard news of reward money. Other people seem to have

Among the many "artifacts" that are likely hoaxes are these fragments of wood said to have washed up on the Alaska shoreline.

made up stories in order to grab their own moment of fame. At least one was intriguing enough to cause Putnam to follow up, but it was a hoax. Finally, he conceded that his wife was gone.

Amy Earhart held out hope for years that her daughter might be alive. She even kept a suitcase ready to go in case news came of her daughter being on an island somewhere. But on January 1, 1939, Amelia Earhart's death was officially declared.

All kinds of theories have been proposed about Amelia's demise. Some people believed that the fliers were captured by the Japanese; there was also the somewhat pervasive claim that Amelia was a spy for the Roosevelt administration. This idea also fed on pre-World War II tensions—and was refueled when the United States became involved in the conflict after the bombing of Pearl Harbor in 1941. This spy conspiracy theory was popularized by a 1943 movie, *Flight to Freedom*, which portrayed a fictional spy pilot that bore striking similarities to Amelia. One theory even had Amelia returning to live out her years as a New Jersey housewife named Irene Bolam.

There have also been many attempts at scientific explanations. The disagreement over which radio frequency Amelia was supposed to be transmitting from has caused confusion. Some others have also said that the maps were partly at fault—that the coordinates of Howland Island were incorrect on the chart Noonan had. But when Anne Pellegreno set out to duplicate Amelia's trip in 1967—the 30th anniversary of the flight—using the same coordinates, Pellegreno found them to be accurate.

Entire books have been devoted to various theories, and some authors have what appears to be well-researched evidence to back up their version of what they believe happened. But it's important to remember that a lot of the information gathered has been from questionable eyewitness accounts and firsthand recollections that are subject to interpretation, as well cloudy memories.

Consider one report that a white man and woman were spotted on Gardner Island (now Nikumaroro) sometime in 1937. It may be perfectly true that *a* couple fitting this description was seen, and that they seemed out of place. But there is nothing conclusive to prove that the couple was Noonan and Amelia. The International Group for Historic Aircraft Recovery (TIGHAR) believes pieces found near the island from an airplane that crashed sometime before 1939 could be from Amelia's plane. Again, there is no proof. As of now, it is impossible to know if there is truth to any of these ideas.

It is most likely, in this biographer's opinion, that the Electra crashed somewhere off-course in the Pacific Ocean. Perhaps the pair missed the tiny Howland Island while flying through a cloud, continuing past it without their knowledge. It seems probable that the Electra went down in the ocean, and that Amelia and Noonan perished not long after.

Many agree this is the most plausible scenario. In 1973, more than 30 years later, talk began of trying to locate the Electra on the ocean floor. In 1989, the Scripps Institution of Oceanography in San Diego, which had the technology to map the ocean floor, took a look at the area near Howland Island. This research showed that the water there averaged 17,250 feet (27,761 km) deep and that there was no underwater mountainous terrain in the area. This meant a sonar search was possible, but between the cost of such an endeavor and the logistical obstacles involved

A group of men stand behind a corner stone for a lighthouse planned on Howland Island to honor Amelia. The memorial was damaged in World War II, and repaired in 1963.

These goggles belonged to Amelia Earhart.

with a midocean expedition, it was not done at the time.

More recent work was undertaken by Nauticos, a company that has spent millions of dollars on underwater sonar research to try and pinpoint the exact location of the Electra. In 2002, they searched more than 600 square miles (966 sq km) of ocean floor off Howland, using deep-sea sonar technology and found nothing. Nauticos has indicated plans to return and continue the search in the future.

Whether or not the mystery of what happened to Amelia Earhart is ever solved, the life she led was—and still is—a source of inspiration. When the news of her disappearance hit the papers, people were devastated. Amy, Muriel, and Putnam all received many letters from strangers grieving their loss. One wrote: "If they are not found I will always think of them as Queen Amelia and King Frederick of some island." Zonta, a women's professional group, and the National Woman's Party established funds in her honor. Ruth Nichols and the Ninety-Nines started the annual Amelia Earhart Memorial Scholarships, which are still given today.

While Amelia made an enormous impact on everyday people, consider also some of

SONAR

Sonar is a method of transmitting and reflecting underwater sound waves in order to locate objects under water or measure underwater distances.

the most influential and famous figures who sang her praises. Eleanor Roosevelt, Ida Tarbell (a journalist known for exposing corruption), and Carrie Chapman Catt (founder of the League of Women Voters) counted her among the most important women of their time. And in fact, one of the most significant things Amelia did was to speak out for the advancement of all women in light of her individual achievements.

Amelia was a wonderful role model, living life as she saw fit instead of conforming to societal ideas of what women should or should not do. She likely inspired countless girls (and women) to reach for their dreams. More literally, several women actually followed in Amelia's high-altitude footsteps. Three years before Anne Pellegreno's 1967 flight, Geraldine Mock succeeded at

Although she died young, Amelia lived her life to the fullest. She is an inspiration to all of us to follow our dreams.

becoming the first woman to fly around the globe. That same year, 1964, Joan Merriam Smith was the first to duplicate Amelia's route.

We may never know what actually happened to Amelia Earhart. What is certain, though, is that she lived her life on her own terms—ferociously. She bucked all the traditional constraints that held back many women of her time, even going so far as to make clear to her fiancé that she did not intend to be a typical housewife. She pushed against obstacles until they gave way, worked toward the greater good, and lived life for the fun of it. She took care of those she loved, took risks, and took the consequences as they fell. She was a role model when she was alive, and remains a role model to this day. Amelia Earhart's bold, colorful life is forever woven into the fabric of our history.

Events in the Life of Amelia Earhart

July 24, 1897
Amelia Earhart is born in Atchison, Kansas.

September 1928
Amelia publishes *20 Hr., 40 Min.*

January 3, 1921
Neta Snook gives Amelia her first flying lesson.

1916
Amelia begins at the Ogontz School.

October 1922
Amelia sets an altitude record for women at 14,000 feet (4,267 m).

February 1918
Amelia becomes a nurse's aid at Spadina Military Hospital in Toronto.

June 3, 1928
Amelia and crew take off on the *Friendship* flight across Atlantic.

December 17, 1903
Orville Wright acheives the first powered, piloted flight.

May 16, 1923
Amelia receives her pilot's license.

February 1931
Amelia marries G.P. Putnam.

1935
Amelia takes a job at Purdue University.

May 21, 1932
Amelia becomes the first woman to make a solo transatlantic flight.

November 1929
The Ninety-Nines women's pilot organization is created.

July 1929
Amelia is hired by Transcontinental Air Transport.

March 17, 1937
Amelia makes her first attempt at her round-the-world trip.

1932
Amelia publishes *The Fun of It*.

April 19, 1935
Amelia sets off on her flight to Mexico.

August 18, 1929
Women's Cross-Country Air Race.

April 1931
Amelia flies the autogiro and sets altitude records in it.

July 3, 1937
Amelia and Noonan disappear.

January 11, 1935
Amelia makes a solo flight from Honolulu, Hawaii, to Oakland, California.

Bibliography

Books

Backus, Jean L. *Letters from Amelia: An Intimate Portrait of Amelia Earhart.* Boston, MA: Beacon Press, 1982.

Brink, Randall. *Lost Star: The Search for Amelia Earhart.* New York: W.W. Norton & Company, 1993.

Butler, Susan. *East to the Dawn: The Life of Amelia Earhart.* New York: Da Capo Press, 1999.

Earhart, Amelia. *The Fun of It: Random Records of My Own Flying and of Women in Aviation.* New York: Harcourt Brace, 1932.

_____. *20 Hrs., 40 Min.: Our Flight in the* Friendship. Washington, D.C.: National Geographic Society, 2001. (reprinted from the original 1928 edition)

Goldstein, Donald M. and Dillon, Katherine V. *Amelia: A Life of the Aviation Legend.* Washington, D.C.: Brassey's, 1997.

Jessen, Gene Nora. *The Powder Puff Derby of 1929.* Naperville, IL: Sourcebooks, Inc., 2002.

King, Thomas F., Jacobson, Randall S., Burns, Karen R. and Spading, Kenton. *Amelia Earhart's Shoes: Is the Mystery Solved?* Walnut Creek, CA: AltaMira Press, 2001.

Long, Elgen M. and Marie K. Long. *Amelia Earhart: The Mystery Solved.* New York: Simon and Schuster, 1999.

Lovell, Mary S. *The Sound of Wings: The Life of Amelia Earhart.* New York: St. Martin's Press, 1989.

Putnam, George Palmer. *Soaring Wings.* New York: Manor Books, 1972.

Rich, Doris L. *Amelia Earhart: A Biography.* Washington, D.C.: Smithsonian Institution Press, 1989.

Shore, Nancy. *Amelia Earhart: Aviator.* New York: Chelsea House, 1987.

Ware, Susan. *Still Missing: Amelia Earhart and the Search for Modern Feminism.* New York: W. W. Norton & Company, 1993.

Films

A&E Biography. *Amelia Earhart: Queen of the Air.* New York: A&E Television Networks, 1996.

Hoffman, David. *Following Amelia Earhart: Heroines of the Sky.* Varied Directions, 2002.

Articles

Lindbergh, Reeve. "Charles Lindbergh." *Time.* June 14, 1999.

Morell, Virginia. "Amelia Earhart." *National Geographic.* Vol. 193, No. 1, pp. 112-135.

Roach, John. "Where is Amelia Earhart? Three Theories." *National Geographic News.* December 15, 2003.

Sources Cited

P 11: "Amelia was more fun..." *East to the Dawn,* 45. P 12: "shocked all the nice little girls" *National Geographic* article "Amelia Earhart." 114. P 13–14: "Had I been sitting up,..." *The Fun of It,* 12. P 15: "It was a thing of rusty wire..." *The Sound of Wings,* 15. P 17: "I have never lived more than four years..." *The Fun of It,* 18. P 19: "Of course I'm going to Bryn Mawr..." *The Sound of Wings,* 18. P 20: "The girl in brown who walks alone." A*melia: A Life of the Aviation Legend,* 20. P 21: "Poppy was such a lamb..." *Letters from Amelia,* 30. P 22: "you know the more one does..." *Letters from Amelia*, 38. P 23: "We others are only asking..." *The Sound of Wings*, 25–26. P 23–24: "men without arms..." *The Fun of It*, 19. P 24: "There is so much that must..." *20 Hrs., 40 Min.*, 5. P 25: "no civilian had opportunity..." *The Fun of It*, 20. P 25: "if something went wrong..." and "I did not understand it at the time..." *East to the Dawn*, 85. P 28–29: "More than once we climbed the endless steps..." "I can think of lots of things.." and "I'll see what I can do..." *Amelia: A Life of the Aviation Legend*, 27, 28. P 31: "As soon as we left the ground..." *The Fun of It*, 25. P 31: "do everything around a plane that a man can do..." *Amelia: A Life of the Aviation Legend*, 31. P 35 "I had not bobbed it..." *The Fun of It*, 26. P 36–37: "There wasn't much..." "This is the day I learn..." and "I think he has the mating instinct..." *Amelia Earhart: A Biography*, 28, 29, 30. P 38: "looked thoroughly feminine..." *East to the Dawn*, 98. P 39: "not a plane for a beginner..." *Letters from Amelia*, 37. P 40: "Like a favorite pony..." *East to the Dawn*, 100. P 41: "I refused to fly alone..." and "I was then introduced to aerobatics..." *20 Hrs., 40 Min.*, 15. P 43: "A Lady's Plane..." *East to the Dawn*, 109. P 43–44: "The minute I flew..." and "I lingered on in California..." *20 Hrs., 40 Min.*, 26, 32. P 46: "It was extraordinarily confusing..." *20 Hrs., 40 Min.*, 30. P 49: "A woman can get by..." *Amelia: A Life of the Aviation Legend*, 33. P 50: "Neither she nor I had ever seen..." *The Fun of It*, 49. P 53: "Experiment!..." *Soaring Wings*, 47. P 54: "To me, one of the biggest jobs of the social worker..." *Soaring Wings*, 49. P 58: "...interested in doing something for aviation..." and "Would you fly the Atlantic?" *The Fun of It*, 59. P 59: "It startles me..." *The Sound of Wings*, 108. P 61–62: "Even though I have lost..." "Hooray for the last grand adventure..." and "I have tried to play for a large stake..." *East to the Dawn*, 170. P 64–65: "because pontoons stick..." *East to the Dawn*, 166. P 67: "A flock of birds..." and "maritime cowboys" *20 Hrs., 40 Min.*, 67,71. P 67: "Wish I were with you." *Amelia: A Life of the Aviation Legend*, 48. P 69: "We are bucking a head wind..." *20 Hrs., 40 Min.*, 96. P 70–71: "8:50. 2 Boats!!!!..." "In the enthusiasm..." and "I tried to make them realize..." *20 Hrs., 40 Min.*, 107, 115. P 71: "I was just baggage..." *Amelia: A Life of the Aviation Legend*, 54. P 73: "More than ever did I then realize..." *Still Missing*, 44. P 74: "they danced..." *Soaring Wings*, 70. P 74: "I'm not interested in you a bit..." *Amelia: A Life of the Aviation Legend*, 59. P 75–76: "I'm afraid my value..." *Amelia: A Life of the Aviation Legend*, 62. P 77: "If you know something..." *East to the Dawn*, 211. P 79: "special responsibility for attracting women..." *The Sound of Wings*, 145. P 81: "It was all the more necessary that we keep on flying." *Amelia: A Life of the Aviation Legend*, 73. P 82–83: "frantically braking and attempting..." and "I was filled with admiration..." *The Sound of Wings*, 151. P 83–84: "To provide a close relationshi.." *East to the Dawn*, 233. P 85: "He looks thinner than I've ever seen him..." *Amelia: A Life of the Aviation Legend*, 74. P 86: "I am no longer engaged..." *The Sound of Wings*, 138. P 88: "I should like the old quilts..." *East to the Dawn*, 253. P 89: "This is an era of feminine activity..." *Still Missing*, 101. P 90: "Would you mind..." "a clutch at the heart" and "something akin to elation..." *Soaring Wings*, 99. P 91–92: "I did my best..." *East to the Dawn*, 269. P 92: "If anyone finds the wreck..." and "small exploit has drawn attention..." *National Geographic* article "Amelia Earhart" 127, 131. P 93: "You beat me to it..." and "Your flight is a splendid success." *Amelia: A Life of the Aviation Legend*, 99. P 95: "Stars hung outside my cockpit window..." *East to the Dawn*, 327. P 95: "I knew she would do it..." *Amelia: A Life of the Aviation Legend*, 133. P 97: "Women must try to do things..." *National Geographic* article "Amelia Earhart" 122. P 97: "I know from practical experience..." *Still Missing*, 124. P 100–101: "It seems to me you've got everything to lose..." *Amelia Earhart: Aviator*, 86. P 101: "Like previous flights,..." *Amelia: A Life of the Aviation Legend*, 158. P 103: "an interesting commentary ..." *Amelia: A Life of the Aviation Legend*, 172. P 105: "at its waistline," *Amelia Earhart: Aviator*, 88. P 105: "There was an almost audible clatter..." and "I have a feeling there is just about one more..." *The Sound of Wings*, 260. P 106: "For a female to be traveling as I do..." and "Have never seen such rain...." *Amelia: A Life of the Aviation Legend*, 193, 196. P 107–108: "the maps of the country..." and "killing time appears to be..." *Amelia: A Life of the Aviation Legend*, 200. P 108: "Better wear your parachute." *East to the Dawn*, 394. P 111: "...the whole width of the world has passed..." *Amelia: A Life of the Aviation Legend*, 223. P 113: "We must be on you..." and "We are running north and south." *Amelia Earhart: The Mystery Solved*, 27, 30. P 119: "If they are not found I will always think of them..." *Still Missing*, 225.

Index

Acknowledgments

Special thanks to Susan Ware, author and historian, for her expert review of this manuscript. I would also like to thank my family, for giving me the time and support needed to be a writer. A, J, and L—you make me soar.

For Further Study

The home where Amelia Earhart lived with her grandparents is now the Amelia Earhart Birthplace Museum in Atchison, Kansas. (http://www.ameliaearhartmuseum.org/home1.htm)

The International Forest of Friendship in Atchison, Kansas, pays tribute to the many past and present heroes of aviation and aerospace. (http://www.ifof.org/index.html)

Visit the 99s Museum of Women Pilots on Amelia Earhart Road in Oklahoma City, Oklahoma. The museum has a wealth of information on the history of female pilots and the role they played in the developing aviation field. (http://www.museamofwomanpilots.com)

Picture Credits

The images in this book are used with permission and through the courtesy of: The Schlesinger Library,Radcliffe Institute, Harvard University: pp. 6, 10, 12, 16, 19, 20, 25, 27, 28, 34, 48, 50T, 90, 95B, 96, 102, 122TC, 123BC. Atchison County Historical Society: pp. 7, 11, 13, 22, 46–47, 49, 85, 103, 120–121, 123BR. Getty Images: pp.8, 33, 42, 44, 65, 73, 100, 123TR, 123BCL. Purdue University Libraries, Archives and Special Collections/Amelia Earhart Collection: pp. 2, 9, 32, 47T, 66, 95T, 108, 109, 110T, 112, 119, 122BR. The State Historical Society of Iowa: p. 14. Library of Congress: pp. 15, 37L, 39, 63, 74, 75, 87, 93, 113, 122BL, 122CR. Minnesota Historical Society: pp. 17, 39. Corbis: pp. 18, 31, 54, 58, 83 Underwood and Underwood; p. 26 Hulton Deutsch; pp. 4–5, 29, 30, 41, 60, 62, 72, 84, 86, 94, 105, 106, 123TCL, Bettman; p. 37R Corbis; pp. 50–51 Anthony Nex; p. 56 Richard T. Nowitz. Kansas State Historical Society: pp. 24, 43, 122CL. Photovault.com: p35 Dick Neville. Dorling Kindersley: p. 36 Dave King; pp. 76, 110–111, 122TR. National Air and Space Museum, Smithsonian Institute: p. 38 (neg.#78-16945); p. 57 (neg.#86-13507); p. 71 (neg.#2006-21916); p. 79 (neg.#2006-21915 TAT, Inc.); p. 82 (neg.#83-2144); p. 88 (neg.#82-11884); p.89 (neg.#85-3357); p. 91 (neg.#2002-3397 Eric.F.Long); p.99 (neg.#72-744); p. 104 (neg.#2006-21919); p. 107 (neg.#71-1060); p. 114 (neg.#2006-21918); p. 115 (neg.#2006-20958); p. 116 (neg.#2006-21917); p. 118 (neg.#71-1057); p. 123TL (neg.#2000-2414); p. 123BL (neg.#2002-3397 Eric F. Long). Cleveland Public Library: pp .40, 45, 68, 69, 81, 92, 97, 98, 123TCR, 123TC, 124, 125, 126, 127. Boston Public Library: pp. 52, 55. Alamy Images: pp. 70 Popperfoto; 80 Digital Archives Japan. Amelia Earhart Museum: p. 122TL. BORDER PICTURES: from left to right: Atchison County Historical Society; Amelia Earhart Museum; Purdue University Libraries, Archives and Special Collections /Amelia Earhart Collection; Dorling Kindersley; Atchison County Historical Society; Library of Congress; Alamy Images/Popperfoto; Getty Images; The Schlesinger Library,Radcliffe Institute, Harvard University; Library of Congress; Purdue University Libraries, Archives and Special Collections/ Amelia Earhart Collection; Purdue University Libraries, Archives and Special Collections /Amelia Earhart Collection.

About the Author

Tanya Lee Stone was an editor for 13 years before becoming a children's author. Since that time, she has been written more than 80 books on topics that include science, nature, history, and biography. She also writes young adult fiction. As a student at Oberlin College, she studied English, creative writing, history, and music. Later, she received a Masters in Education. Stone often travels to schools and talks about books with young people. To learn more, visit www.tanyastone.com.

Other DK Biographies you'll enjoy:

Albert Einstein
by Frieda Wishinsky
ISBN 978-0-7566-1247-4 paperback
ISBN 978-0-7566-1248-1 hardcover

Princess Diana
by Joanne Mattern
ISBN 978-0-7566-1614-4 paperback
ISBN 978-0-7566-1613-7 hardcover

Helen Keller
by Leslie Garrett
ISBN 978-0-7566-0339-7 paperback
ISBN 978-0-7566-0488-2 hardcover

Eleanor Roosevelt
by Kem Knapp Sawyer
ISBN 978-0-7566-1496-6 paperback
ISBN 978-0-7566-1495-9 hardcover

Gandhi
by Amy Pastan
ISBN 978-0-7566-2111-7 paperback
ISBN 978-0-7566-2112-4 hardcover

George Washington
by Lenny Hort
ISBN 978-0-7566-0835-4 paperback
ISBN 978-0-7566-0832-3 hardcover

John F. Kennedy
by Howard S. Kaplan
ISBN 978-0-7566-0340-3 paperback
ISBN 978-0-7566-0489-9 hardcover

Nelson Mandela
by Laaren Brown & Lenny Hort
ISBN 978-0-7566-2109-4 paperback
ISBN 978-0-7566-2110-0 hardcover

Martin Luther King, Jr.
by Amy Pastan
ISBN 978-0-7566-0342-7 paperback
ISBN 978-0-7566-0491-2 hardcover

Harry Houdini
by Vicki Cobb
ISBN 978-0-7566-1245-0 paperback
ISBN 978-0-7566-1246-7 hardcover

Charles Darwin
by David C. King
ISBN 978-0-7566-2554-2 paperback
ISBN 978-0-7566-2555-9 hardcover

Abraham Lincoln
by Tanya Lee Stone
ISBN 978-0-7566-0834-7 paperback
ISBN 978-0-7566-0833-0 hardcover

Look what the critics are saying about DK Biography!

"…highly readable, worthwhile overviews for young people…"—*Booklist*

"This new series from the inimitable DK Publishing brings together the usual brilliant photography with a historian's approach to biography subjects."
—*Ingram Library Services*